JON KRAKAUER

THREE CUPS OF DECEIT

Jon Krakauer is the author of eight books and
has received an Academy Award in Literature
from the American Academy of Arts and
Letters. According to the award citation,
"Krakauer combines the tenacity and courage of
the finest tradition of investigative journalism
with the stylish subtlety and profound insight of
the born writer."

www.jonkrakauer.com

Also by Jon Krakauer

Eiger Dreams
Into the Wild
Into Thin Air
Under the Banner of Heaven
Where Men Win Glory
Missoula
Classic Krakauer

THREE CUPS · of · DECEIT

*How Greg Mortenson,
Humanitarian Hero,
Lost His Way*

Revised and Updated Edition

JON KRAKAUER

Anchor Books
A Division of Penguin Random House LLC
New York

SECOND ANCHOR BOOKS EDITION, NOVEMBER 2014

Copyright © 2011, 2014 by Jon Krakauer

All rights reserved. Published in the United States by
Anchor Books, a division of Penguin Random House LLC,
New York, and distributed in Canada by Random House of
Canada, a division of Penguin Random House Canada Limited,
Toronto. Originally published digitally, in somewhat different
form, in the United States by Byliner, Inc., in 2011.

Anchor Books and colophon are registered trademarks of
Penguin Random House LLC.

The Cataloging-in-Publication Data is on file at the Library of
Congress.

Anchor Books Trade Paperback ISBN: 978-0-307-94876-2

www.anchorbooks.com

Printed in the United States of America
12   11   10   9

CONTENTS

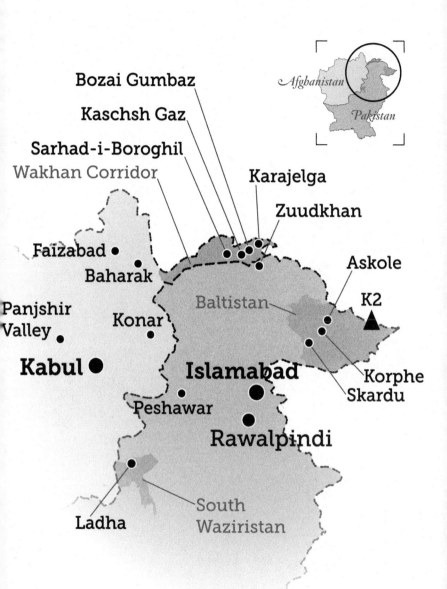

Bozai Gumbaz

Kaschsh Gaz

Sarhad-i-Boroghil

Wakhan Corridor

Karajelga

Zuudkhan

Faizabad

Baharak

Askole

K2

Panjshir
Valley

Konar

Baltistan

Kabul

Islamabad

Korphe

Skardu

Peshawar

Rawalpindi

Ladha

South
Waziristan

Afghanistan

Pakistan

DRAMATIS PERSONAE

Greg Mortenson: Executive director and co-founder of the Central Asia Institute (CAI); co-author of *Three Cups of Tea*; author of *Stones into Schools*

David Oliver Relin: Co-author of *Three Cups of Tea*, who died in 2012

Christa Mortenson: Greg's youngest sister, who died in 1992

Mouzafer Ali: Resident of Pakistan's Baltistan region whom Mortenson hired to carry his backpack from the base of K2 to the village of Askole in September 1993

Haji Ali: Chieftain of a Balti village called Korphe, located across the Braldu River from Askole

Scott Darsney: Greg Mortenson's climbing partner on K2 in 1993

Yakub: Friend of Mouzafer Ali whom Darsney hired to carry his backpack from the base of K2 to the village of Askole in 1993

Akhmalu: Expedition cook for Greg Mortenson and his teammates on K2 in 1993; shortly after the expedition ended, Mortenson visited Akhmalu's village, Khane, and promised to build a school there

Erica Stone: President of the American Himalayan Foundation

Jean Hoerni: Theoretical physicist and co-founder of CAI who gave Greg Mortenson $12,000 in 1994 to build his first school in Pakistan, and in 1996 donated $1 million to CAI; he died in 1997

Mohammed Ali Changazi: Tour operator and trekking agent who managed the logistics for Mortenson's 1993 K2 expedition; adopted son of Haji Ali

Tara Bishop: Greg Mortenson's wife, a clinical psychologist; the daughter of mountaineer Barry Bishop

Naimat Gul Mahsud: A member of the Mahsud tribe who met Mortenson in the Pakistani city of Rawalpindi in July 1996 and, at Mortenson's request, drove him to Ladha, South

Waziristan, the Mahsud ancestral homeland, where he was Mortenson's host

Mansur Khan Mahsud: Director of research at the FATA Research Centre who accompanied Mortenson on sightseeing excursions in South Waziristan in July 1996, during the period Mortenson claims the Taliban held him captive

Hussein Mohammed: Pseudonym of a member of the Mahsud tribe who is acquainted with Naimat Gul Mahsud

Jennifer Wilson: Jean Hoerni's third wife, who served on the CAI board of directors from 1997 to 2001

Tom Vaughan: Chairman of CAI's board of directors, 1997–2001

Tom Hornbein: American physician and mountaineer renowned for making the first ascent of the West Ridge of Mount Everest in 1963; invited to join the CAI board in 1999, he became its chairman in 2001 and resigned in 2002

Barry Bishop: Tara Bishop's father; Tom Hornbein's teammate on Everest in 1963

Gordon Wiltsie: Eminent photographer and mountaineer, member of the CAI board of directors, 1998–2002

Sally Uhlmann: Businesswoman and member of the CAI board of directors, 2000–2002

King Zaher Shah: King of Afghanistan 1933–1973, who died in 2007

Sadhar Khan: Powerful warlord, or *qomandan*, in the northern Afghanistan province of Badakhshan

Mostapha Zaher: Grandson of King Zaher Shah

Debbie Raynor: Chief financial officer of CAI, 2003–2004

Daniel Borochoff: President of the American Institute of Philanthropy, a charity watchdog organization

Ghulam Parvi: CAI's program manager in Pakistan, 1996–June 2010; one of Mortenson's "Dirty Dozen"

Tanya Rosen: Wildlife researcher and international lawyer who has conducted extensive research in Baltistan

Kate DeClerk: CAI's international program director, 2003–2004

Mike Bryan: Journalist Mortenson hired to ghostwrite an early draft of *Stones into Schools*

Kevin Fedarko: Journalist who wrote "He Fights Terror With Books," the 2003 *Parade* magazine article that established Mortenson's reputation; second ghostwriter of *Stones into Schools*

Roshan Khan: Kyrgyz horseman whom Mortenson purportedly promised, in 1999, to build a school in Bozai Gumbaz

Abdul Rashid Khan: Supreme leader of the Afghan Kyrgyz people whom Mortenson met in the Afghan city of Baharak in 2005; the father of Roshan Khan, he died in 2009

Ted Callahan: American anthropologist and mountaineer Mortenson hired in 2006 to write a report about the feasibility of building a school for Kyrgyz nomads in northeastern Afghanistan's remote Wakhan Corridor

Sarfraz Khan: Pakistani who oversaw CAI's programs in northern Pakistan and northern Afghanistan; one of Mortenson's "Dirty Dozen," he died of cancer in 2012

Whitney Azoy: Cultural anthropologist who has spent many years working in Afghanistan; Ted Callahan's friend and mentor

Colonel Ilyas Mirza: Retired Pakistani military officer who served as CAI's chief operations director in Islamabad until 2013; one of Mortenson's "Dirty Dozen"

Haji Osman: Kyrgyz chieftain in the Afghan Pamir, near the Bozai Gumbaz school

Ghial Beg: Headman of an Afghan village named Kret in the Wakhan Corridor, where CAI built a school

Steve Bullock: Montana attorney general whose investigation of Mortenson and CAI exposed numerous "financial transgressions" and "serious internal problems in the management of CAI"

Anne Beyersdorfer: Public relations specialist who served as interim executive director of CAI when Mortenson took a paid leave of absence in April 2011

David Starnes: Executive director of CAI appointed to replace Beyersdorfer in March 2013 after she was forced to resign in the aftermath of Montana attorney general Bullock's investigation. Starnes abruptly resigned from CAI in May 2014

Suleman Minhas: Ex–taxi driver who oversees CAI's programs in the Pakistani Punjab; one of Mortenson's "Dirty Dozen"

Farhan Jamal Akhtar: Finance manager for the CAI Trust in Pakistan who blew the whistle on the corrupt management of the trust by Ilyas Mirza

Jennifer Sipes: CAI operations director

Twaha: Son of Korphe chieftain Haji Ali

PREFACE TO THE REVISED AND UPDATED EDITION

On April 17, 2011, the television news program *60 Minutes* broadcast an exposé of Greg Mortenson and his celebrated charity, the Central Asia Institute. Correspondent Steve Kroft revealed "serious questions about how millions of dollars have been spent, whether Mortenson is personally benefiting, and whether some of the most dramatic and inspiring stories in his books are even true." A day later, Byliner published the first edition of *Three Cups of Deceit*, which corroborated the charges made by *60 Minutes*, and revealed significantly more wrongdoing than Kroft was able to report in a fifteen-minute television segment.

Because Mortenson resides in Bozeman, Montana, and his charity's headquarters is also there, the allegations made by *60 Minutes* and me attracted the attention of Montana attorney general Steve Bullock. He launched an investigation of Mortenson and his organization, documenting numerous "financial transgressions" and "serious internal problems in the management of CAI." Mortenson was ultimately ordered to pay CAI $1.2 million in restitution for funds he'd misappropriated, including $214,000 he charged to CAI "for such things as L.L. Bean clothing, iTunes, luggage, luxurious accommodations, and even vacations."

But even after Mortenson was unmasked as a self-aggrandizing fabulist who used CAI as his personal cash machine, he adroitly leveraged the allegiance of steadfast supporters on the CAI board of directors to maintain control over the charity. As a consequence, the board continues to present Mortenson as CAI's moral exemplar and guiding light, and still pays him $169,000 per year. This is no small triumph for Mortenson, given the voluminous and irrefutable evidence of his misdemeanors.

Mortenson's success at dodging accountability can be explained in part by the self-effacing, Mother Teresa–like image he presents for public consumption. But it also demonstrates how difficult it is to correct a false belief after people have made an emotional investment in that belief being true. When our heroes turn out to be sleazebags, self-deception is easier than facing the facts.

Mortenson has granted many hundreds of media interviews over the years, tirelessly promoting his charity and himself. But he declined multiple requests from both me and *60 Minutes* to be interviewed in 2011, and shortly after the scandal broke, he went underground and refused to answer questions from journalists or donors, choosing instead to communicate sporadically through spokespersons. Many of these communiqués have been evasive or untrue.

Mortenson finally ended his nearly three-year media embargo in January 2014 when he agreed to be interviewed by Tom Brokaw on the *Today* show. Mortenson didn't use the opportunity to come clean, however. Instead, he looked Brokaw in the eye and doubled down on his claim that his books are truthful accounts. "I stand by the stories," he insisted. "The stories happened."

Mortenson has changed crucial details of these stories several times since April 2011, improvising on the fly with the instincts of a natural con artist, boldly layering lie upon lie to confound his inquisitors. One might think this periodic rescripting would eventually catch up to him, but the tactic appears to have worked pretty well thus far. Oversight of the nonprofit sector is lax. It's not hard to game the system. And when hagiographic fables about Potemkin heroes like Mortenson become lodged in the popular imagination, they acquire a sheen of legitimacy that makes them tough to debunk.

After the first edition of *Three Cups of Deceit* was published, I'd intended to move on to other writing projects. But because Mortenson and CAI have continued to deny the truth, and have lately been trying to reinvigorate the cult of personality that contributed to so many of the organization's current woes, I felt duty-bound to stay on the beat and refute the false claims.

This vastly expanded edition of my original report

includes updates large and small throughout, but the bulk of the new material can be found in the 11,000-word afterword. It includes a detailed look at further financial improprieties, and an analysis of recent assertions by Mortenson that he is the innocent victim of a smear campaign by *60 Minutes* and me. My investigation has been buttressed substantially by new sources in Pakistan, Afghanistan, and the United States who've provided fresh evidence that CAI continues to suffer from a deeply ingrained culture of corruption.

My aim in publishing this updated edition is to alert CAI donors to the charity's ongoing problems, and to help the leaders of CAI recognize that these problems will be impossible to solve unless they stop concealing them.

—Jon Krakauer
October 2014

• *Part I* •

THE
CREATION
MYTH

"When it comes right down to it
I am nothing more than a fellow who took
a wrong turn in the mountains and
never quite managed to find his way home."

—GREG MORTENSON,
STONES INTO SCHOOLS

GREG MORTENSON DOESN'T HIDE his light under a bushel. He makes more than 160 public appearances annually, in all parts of the country and abroad, and frequently appears in the news. For each of the past three years he has been nominated for the Nobel Peace Prize. President Obama donated $100,000 of the award money from his own Nobel Peace Prize, which he received in 2009, to the Central Asia Institute (CAI)—the charity Mortenson launched fifteen years ago to build schools in Pakistan and Afghanistan. Visiting classrooms wherever he goes, Mortenson has persuaded 2,800 American schools to become fundraising partners; last year, schoolkids collecting "Pennies for Peace" boosted CAI revenues by $2.5 million. All told, his vigorous promotion of the Greg Mortenson brand generated $23 million in donations to CAI in 2010 alone.

On March 29 of this year, I attended a lecture Mortenson gave in Cheyenne, Wyoming. As he walked onto the stage in the sold-out arena, more than two thousand men, women, and children leapt to their feet to express their admiration with cheers, whistles, and deafening applause. "If we really want to help people, we have to empower people," Mortenson pronounced. "And empowering people starts with education." A book cover depicting Afghan girls engrossed in study was projected onto the screen above the stage. "So I wrote this book called *Three Cups of Tea*," he deadpanned. "Some of you might have heard about it..."

Laughter rippled through the crowd. Hoping to get an autograph from Mortenson, hundreds of fans were holding copies of his book, which had spent the previous four years and two months on the *New York Times* paperback nonfiction bestseller list, and showed every sign of remaining there well into the future. Some five million copies are now in print, including special editions for "young readers" and "very young readers" (kindergarten through fourth grade). Moreover, the multitudes who have bought *Three Cups* haven't merely read it; they've embraced it with singular passion. Since its publication in 2006, people galvanized by this autobiographical account of Mortenson's school-building adventures have donated more than $50 million to the Central Asia Institute. The book's popularity stems from its forceful, uncomplicated theme—terrorism can be eradicated by educating children in impoverished societies—and its portrayal of Mortenson as a humble, Gandhi-like figure who has repeatedly risked life and limb to advance his humanitarian agenda.

Told in the third person by Mortenson's co-author, David Oliver Relin, *Three Cups* begins with Mortenson hiking down Pakistan's Baltoro Glacier in September 1993, having failed to climb K2, the second-highest peak on earth. A trauma nurse by profession, he'd been invited to join an expedition to K2 to serve as the team medic.[1] After two months of punishing effort, however, Mortenson realized he lacked the strength to reach the summit, so he abandoned his attempt and left the expedition early. Exhausted and dejected, the thirty-five-year-old mountaineer reached into a pocket as he trudged down the trail and "fingered the necklace of amber beads that his little sister Christa had often worn. As a three-year-old in Tanzania, where Mortenson's Minnesota-born parents had been Lutheran missionaries and teachers, Christa had contracted acute meningitis and never fully recovered. Greg, twelve years her senior, had appointed himself her protector."

In July 1992, at age twenty-three, Christa had suffered a massive epileptic seizure, apparently stemming from her childhood health problems, and died. Ten months later, Mortenson had trekked into the Karakoram Range with Christa's necklace, intending to leave it on K2's 28,267-foot summit, which is considerably more difficult to reach than the crest of Mount Everest. Now the defeated Mortenson "wiped his eyes with his sleeve, disoriented by the unfamiliar tears.... After seventy-eight days of primal struggle at altitude on K2, he felt like a faint, shriveled caricature of himself." He wasn't even sure he had the strength to make it to Askole, the village at trail's end, fifty miles down the valley.

A week into his homeward trek through Baltistan, as this corner of Pakistan is known, Mortenson became separated from Mouzafer Ali, the Balti porter he had hired to carry his heavy backpack. Without Mouzafer's guidance, Mortenson took a wrong turn and lost his way. A few hours later, he arrived at a village he assumed was Askole. As Mortenson walked into the settlement, a throng of local youngsters, fascinated by the tall foreigner, gathered around him. "By the time he reached the village's ceremonial entrance...he was leading a procession of fifty children."

Just beyond, Mortenson was greeted warmly by "a wizened old man, with features so strong they might have been carved out of the canyon walls." His name was Haji Ali, the village chieftain. He led Mortenson to his stone hut, "placed cushions at the spot of honor closest to the open hearth, and installed Mortenson there.... When Mortenson looked up, he saw the eyes of the fifty children who had followed him," peering down from a large square opening in the roof. "Here, warm by the hearth, on soft pillows, snug in the crush of so much humanity, he felt the exhaustion he'd been holding at arm's length surge up over him."

At that moment, though, Haji Ali revealed to Mortenson that he wasn't in Askole, as the American believed. Owing to his wrong turn, he'd blundered into a village called Korphe. "Adrenaline snapped Mortenson back upright. He'd never heard of Korphe.... Rousing himself, he explained that he had to get to Askole and meet a man named Mouzafer who was carrying all his belongings. Haji Ali gripped his guest by the shoulders with his powerful hands and pushed him back on the pillows." Surrendering to fatigue, Mortenson closed his eyes and sank into a deep sleep.

In *Three Cups of Tea*, Mortenson never indicates exactly how many days he spent in Korphe on that initial visit in 1993, but he implies it was a lengthy stay:

> From his base in Haji Ali's home, Mortenson settled into a routine. Each morning and afternoon he would walk briefly about Korphe, accompanied, as always, by children tugging at his hands.... Off the Baltoro, out of danger, he realized just how precious his own survival had been, and how weakened he'd become. He could barely make it down the switchback

path that led to the river.... Wheezing his way back up to the village, he felt as infirm as the elderly men who sat for hours at a time under Korphe's apricot trees, smoking from hookahs and eating apricot kernels. After an hour or two of poking about each day he'd succumb to exhaustion and return to stare at the sky from his nest of pillows by Haji Ali's hearth.

During his protracted recuperation in Korphe, Mortenson became aware of the Baltis' poverty, and "how close they lived to hunger." He noticed the widespread malnutrition and disease, and learned that one out of every three Korphe children perished before their first birthday. "Mortenson couldn't imagine discharging the debt he felt to his hosts in Korphe. But he was determined to try." He gave away most of his possessions, including his camping stove and warm expedition clothing.

Each day, as he grew stronger, he spent long hours climbing the steep paths between Korphe's homes, doing what little he could to beat back the avalanche of need.... He set broken bones and did what little he could with painkillers and antibiotics. Word of his work spread and the sick on the outskirts of Korphe began sending relatives to fetch "Dr. Greg," as he would thereafter be known in northern Pakistan....

Often during his time in Korphe, Mortenson felt the presence of his little sister Christa, especially when he was with Korphe's children.... They reminded [him] of the way Christa had to fight for the simplest things. Also the way she had of just persevering, no matter what life threw at her. He decided he wanted to do something for them.... Lying by the hearth before bed, Mortenson told Haji Ali he wanted to visit Korphe's school.

The following morning, "after their familiar breakfast of *chapattis* and *cha*,"

Haji Ali led Mortenson up a steep path to a vast open ledge.... He was appalled to see eighty-two children, seventy-eight boys and the four girls who had the pluck to join them, kneeling in the frosty ground, in the open. Haji Ali, avoiding Mortenson's eyes, said that the village had no school, and the Pakistani government didn't provide a teacher.... Mortenson watched, his heart in his throat, as the students stood at rigid attention and began their 'school day' with Pakistan's national anthem.... After the last note of the anthem had faded, the children sat in a neat circle and began copying their multiplication tables. Most scratched in the dirt with a stick they'd brought for that purpose.

"I felt like my heart was being torn out," Mortenson declares in this passage. "There was a fierceness in their desire to learn, despite how mightily everything was stacked against them, that reminded me of Christa. I knew I had to do something." As Mortenson stood beside Haji Ali that crisp autumn morning, gazing up at the towering peaks of the Karakoram,

climbing K2 to place a necklace on its summit suddenly felt beside the point. There was a much more meaningful gesture he could make in honor of his sister's memory. He put his hands on Haji Ali's shoulders, as the old man had done to him dozens of times since they'd shared their first cup of tea. "I'm going to build you a school," he said, not yet realizing that with those words, the path of his life had just detoured down another trail, a route far more serpentine and arduous than the wrong turns he'd taken since retreating from K2. "I *will* build a school," Mortenson said. "I promise."

This, in Mortenson's dramatic telling, is how he came to dedicate his life to building schools in Pakistan and Afghanistan. He devotes nearly a third of the book to this transformative experience, which he says occurred in September 1993. It's a compelling creation myth, one that he has repeated in thousands of public appearances and media interviews. The problem is, it's precisely that: a myth.

Mortenson didn't really stumble into Korphe after taking a wrong turn on his way down from K2. He wasn't lovingly nursed back to health in the home of Haji Ali. He set no villagers' broken bones. There are no apricot trees in Korphe. On that crisp September morning, shortly before returning to America, Mortenson did not put his hands on Haji Ali's shoulders and promise to build a school. In fact, Mortenson would not even make the acquaintance of Haji Ali, or anyone else in Korphe, until more than a year later, in October 1994, under entirely different circumstances.

The first eight chapters of *Three Cups of Tea* are an intricately wrought work of fiction presented as fact. And by no means was this an isolated act of deceit. It turns out that Mortenson's books and public statements are permeated with falsehoods. The image of Mortenson that has been created for public consumption is an artifact born of fantasy, audacity, and an apparently insatiable hunger for esteem. Mortenson has lied about the noble deeds he has done, the risks he has taken, the people he has met, the number of schools he has built. *Three Cups of Tea* has much in common with *A Million Little Pieces*, the infamous autobiography by James Frey that was exposed as a sham. But Frey, unlike Mortenson, didn't use his phony memoir to solicit tens of millions of dollars in donations from unsuspecting readers, myself among them. Moreover, Mortenson's charity, the Central Asia Institute, has issued fraudulent financial statements, and he has misused millions of dollars donated by schoolchildren and other trusting devotees. "Greg," says a former treasurer of the organization's board of directors, "regards CAI as his personal ATM."

★   ★   ★

THIS IS WHAT ACTUALLY HAPPENED after Mortenson abandoned his attempt on K2. He trekked down from the mountain in the company of three companions: his American friend and climbing partner Scott Darsney; his Balti porter, Mouzafer; and Darsney's porter, Yakub. According to each of these companions, the four men walked together into Askole on the same afternoon, whereupon they immediately hired a jeep to take them to the city of Skardu, the district capital. When they drove out of the mountains, Darsney assured me, Mortenson "didn't know Korphe existed."

Upon their arrival in Skardu, Mouzafer and Yakub quickly departed for their village in the Hushe Valley, a twelve-hour drive to the east, while Mortenson and Darsney stayed in Skardu. They booked a room at the K2 Motel, a comfortable lodge renowned among Western climbers and trekkers for its hospitality and excellent food. After relaxing there for the better part of a week to recuperate from their debilitating expedition, according to Darsney, he and Mortenson hired a jeep to take them to the village of Khane, in the Hushe Valley, the home of their expedition cook, Akhmalu, who had become a friend during the months they'd spent together on K2. The two Americans stayed in Khane for several days as Akhmalu's guest, and Mortenson developed great affection for the residents of the village. When Mortenson learned they had no school, he promised Akhmalu he would return to Khane the following year and build one. Then Mortenson and Darsney departed for Islamabad (via a leisurely sightseeing detour that included Peshawar and the Khyber Pass) to catch a flight home.

Back in the States, Mortenson lived in the San Francisco Bay Area and supported himself as a nurse. In his spare time, he tried to raise money for what he'd christened the Khane School Project. Erica Stone, the director of the American Himalayan Foundation (AHF), remembers "when Greg appeared at my AHF door one day after his K2 expedition and wanted kind of vaguely to do something good." Stone mentored him, encouraged him, and steered him toward potential donors. "I jokingly called him my science experiment," she says, "because he was around so much."

After nearly a year of fundraising, Mortenson had little to show for his efforts until the summer of 1994, when Stone included a short article by Mortenson in the American Himalayan Foundation newsletter. "I came to Hushe as part of an expedition to K2 in 1993," he wrote.

> After seventy days on the mountain, I spent some time in Khane. When I asked to see the school, the villagers took me up to a dusty apricot grove on a hill behind the village. A group of 85 children, five to twelve years old, were sitting in the dirt, reciting spelling tables.... Despite abject poverty, their spirits soared. It was obvious that these children were intensely loved by their community, that their well-being was a top priority. But the village simply had no money for education or health care.... So I made the commitment to help realize a school and clinic in Khane.
>
> I started this project because I care deeply about these people. Two years ago, my youngest sister Christa died suddenly after a valiant 23-year struggle with epilepsy. During her short life, her joyful spirit touched many people, especially me. The Khane School Project is my way of honoring her. If you'd like to be part of this project, please give us a call.

Upon reading the article, a wealthy AHF supporter named Jean Hoerni gave Mortenson $12,000—enough, by Greg's estimation, to build a simple five-room school building in Khane. In October 1994, Mortenson flew to Pakistan, purchased $8,000 worth of lumber and cement in Rawalpindi, and then hired a garishly decorated "jingle" truck to transport everything up the Karakoram Highway to Skardu. There, the building materials were unloaded at a compound owned by Mohammed Ali Changazi, the tour operator and trekking agent who had managed the logistics for Mortenson's K2 expedition the previous year. When Mortenson arrived in Skardu that fall, he intended to build the school in Khane village, as he'd pledged to Akhmalu. And when Mortenson flew back to California seven weeks later, he apparently still intended to fulfill his pledge to build the school in Khane. But during Mortenson's next trip to Pakistan, in March 1995, he was persuaded to abruptly change his plans by an elderly, gnome-like man named Haji Ali, Changazi's adoptive father, who happened to be the chief of a village called Korphe. Until Changazi introduced Mortenson to Haji Ali, Mortenson was unaware of the village.

Haji Ali had learned from Changazi that the starry-eyed American intended to build a school in Khane. When he heard Mortenson was in Pakistan, Haji Ali traveled to Skardu intending to convince him to build the school in *his* village, Korphe, instead. Toward that end, Haji Ali invited Mortenson to come to Korphe as his guest. During Mortenson's brief visit to the village, Haji Ali showered him with Balti hospitality and did his utmost to persuade Mortenson that Korphe was the ideal location for his school.

Haji Ali's lobbying campaign was effective. By the time Mortenson bid adieu to his new best friend, he'd not only decided to renege on the pledge he'd made to the residents of Khane and build the school in Korphe, but he also promised to construct a suspension bridge across the raging Braldu River to connect Korphe to Askole. Although Korphe was just a stone's throw from Askole, directly across the narrow Braldu Gorge, the only way to travel from Korphe to Askole and the world beyond was by riding high above the river in a "rickety box suspended from a cable," as Mortenson describes the primitive conveyance in *Three Cups of Tea*. After Haji Ali extracted a promise from Mortenson to construct the school, he pointed out that unless his American patron first built a bridge to replace the sketchy, hand-operated tram, it would be all but impossible to transport lumber and other building materials across the river.

Mortenson announced his dramatic change of plans in a fax he sent from Skardu soon after his visit to Korphe:

FROM: GREG MORTENSON
     KHANE SCHOOL PROJECT

TO: AMERICAN HIMALAYAN FOUNDATION
     BOARD OF DIRECTORS

DATE: MARCH 19, 1995

RE: RELOCATION OF PROJECT SITE

DEAR BOARD OF DIRECTORS:

SALAAM AND GREETINGS.

FIRST OF ALL, THE PROJECT IS PROGRESSING WELL, I
AM PLEASED TO REPORT.... AFTER MANY WEEKS, I AM
HIGHLY RECOMMENDING MOVING THE PROJECT SITE
TO KORPHE VILLAGE (SEE MAP). KORPHE IS ACROSS THE
BRALDU RIVER FROM ASKOLE....

THESE ARE THE REASONS FOR MY RECOMMENDING
THE TRANSFER OF SITE:

1. NON COOPERATION OF THE KHANE VILLAGE
   HEADMAN/ELDER
2. CORRUPT CONTRACTOR IN HUSHE/KHAPLU
   REGION
3. KORPHE HAS HAD A FULLTIME VOLUNTEER
   TEACHER FOR FIVE YEARS, MARRIED AND WITH
   FAMILY ALL FROM KORPHE
4. THE KORPHE VILLAGE HEADMAN (NURMA
   DTHAR) HAS GIVEN HIS WORD OF HONOR, THE
   SACRIFICE OF A RAM UPON THE SCHOOL LAND, AS
   AN OFFERING OF HIS VILLAGE IN THANKS TO
   ALLAH. THIS MEANS MORE TO A MUSLIM THAN
   ANY PIECE OF PAPER.
5. KORPHE IS HIGHLY VISIBLE. EVERY TREK,
   EXPEDITION AND ARMY CARAVAN TO ENTER THE
   BALTORO/BIAFO WILL PASS BY OUR SCHOOL.

TO BUILD A SCHOOL IN KORPHE, WE WILL NEED TO
BUILD A STEEL CABLE SUSPENSION BRIDGE ACROSS
THE BRALDU TO KORPHE.... THE COST OF THE BRIDGE
WILL BE ABOUT $10,000, WHICH I WILL RAISE ON MY
OWN. I HOPE TO BEGIN BUILDING BY MAY 1995....

FAITHFULLY SUBMITTED,
GREG

This fax is the first document of any kind in which
Mortenson mentions Korphe, and it contradicts many of the
heartwarming details recounted in the first hundred pages of
Three Cups of Tea. A passage on page 97, for example, describes
Mortenson's triumphant "return" to Korphe in 1994, in which
Mortenson, looking Haji Ali in the eye, declares, "I came back
to keep my promise." In fact, Mortenson never set foot in

Korphe until March 1995, and rather than keeping a promise, he was breaking the vow he had made to Khane. On page 89, Mortenson adds insult to this injury when he chastises the Khane villagers, "I never made any promise"—and accuses them of being greedy shysters for trying to hold him to the pledge he'd made in his sister's name—a commitment memorialized in the article he'd written a few months previously.

★　★　★

IN SEPTEMBER 1995, Greg met a lovely, outgoing woman named Tara Bishop, with whom he felt a rare and immediate attachment. Six days later they married. Construction of the Korphe school began in May 1996, under Mortenson's watchful eye. At the beginning of July, when the school walls were standing but the roof framing was not yet complete, Mortenson departed Korphe to spend time with Tara, who had remained in the United States and was seven months pregnant with their first child. Upon flying from Skardu to Islamabad, though, Mortenson impulsively decided to postpone the next leg of his journey home after a chance encounter with a convivial Pashtun named Naimat Gul Mahsud.

Naimat Gul remembers meeting Mortenson outside the latter's hotel in the city of Rawalpindi, a couple of miles from the Islamabad airport: "It was just after dawn. There were light rain showers, and a cool breeze was blowing.... I saw a person making videos, and he suddenly turned his face towards me and waved his hand." A friendly conversation ensued. When Naimat Gul proudly explained that he was a member of the indomitable Mahsud tribe and hailed from South Waziristan Agency, a region strictly off-limits to foreigners, Mortenson's "face filled with curiousness," Naimat Gul recalls, "and he said he was anxious to visit. He asked me if this was possible. I said, 'Yes, why not? You may go with me if you are seriously intended.'... I briefed him that he would be bound not to tell any government official," lest Mortenson be arrested for illegally entering the Federally Administered Tribal Areas, or FATA.

Naimat Gul later sent me a handwritten card from Mortenson confirming their plan to embark on the long drive to Naimat Gul's ancestral homeland on July 13, 1996, in a Toyota Corolla that Naimat Gul had rented. After spending their first night together in Peshawar, Mortenson and Naimat Gul hit the road again early on July 14, crossing the border into the forbidden tribal areas at midday. As they continued driving west and then south, the flat, barren earth rose into a labyrinth of high ridges bristling with thorn-studded oaks. It was a rugged landscape, but a lovely one—somewhat reminiscent of the country around Bozeman, Montana, where four months earlier Greg and Tara had moved to raise a family. Late in the afternoon, Mortenson and Naimat Gul passed from North Waziristan into South Waziristan, and as the sun went down they arrived in Tehsil Ladha, Naimat Gul's home turf (a *tehsil* is a Pakistani administrative division roughly analogous to an American county).

Little did Naimat Gul know, when he offered to take Mortenson to his village and serve as his host and guardian there, that his amiable guest would one day write a book in which their pleasant sojourn would be transformed into an elaborate tale of abduction and intimidation at the hands of murderous *jihadis*—an account that fills an entire chapter of *Three Cups of Tea* (pages 154–173) and that Mortenson has repeated in hundreds of media interviews.

In most of these interviews, Mortenson has distilled the story into an attention-grabbing sound bite. During an appearance on *CBS Evening News* on October 23, 2008, for example, he said of the experience, "I was kidnapped for eight days in Waziristan by the Taliban." In a two-minute promotional video posted on the website of his book publisher, Penguin, Mortenson was slightly more loquacious: "I got kidnapped by the Taliban for eight days.... It was quite a frightening experience. The first three days, all I could think about is they might take me outside at any moment and finish me off."

In *Three Cups of Tea*, however, where he had room to get creative, Mortenson spun a long, fantastical yarn festooned with enthralling details. In this account, Mortenson first encountered Naimat Gul Mahsud in the treacherous city of Peshawar rather than Rawalpindi (where the two men actually met), and Naimat Gul's name was changed to "Mr. Khan." Just before sunset, they arrived in Ladha, South Waziristan, and "Khan" parked his gray Toyota inside a warehouse for the night.

> The scene inside the warehouse set Mortenson immediately on edge. Six Wazir men with bandoliers criss-crossed on their chests slumped on packing crates smoking hashish from a multinecked hookah. Piled against the walls, Mortenson saw stacks of bazookas, rocket-propelled grenade launchers, and crates of oily new AK-47s....
>
> Khan and the elder of the gang, a tall man with rose-colored aviator glasses and a thick black mustache that perched, batlike, on his upper lip, talked heatedly in Pashto about what to do with the outsider for the evening. After they'd finished, [Khan] took a long draw from the hookah and turned to Mortenson. "Haji Mirza please to invite you to his house," he said, smoke dribbling through his teeth.

The fictional Haji Mirza, the fellow with the batlike mustache, lived in a hilltop compound where a "gun tower rose fifty feet above the courtyard so snipers could pick off anyone approaching uninvited." After a meal of roast lamb, during which the Wazir tribesmen "attacked it with their long daggers, stripping tender meat from the bone and cramming it into their mouths with the blades of their knives," Mortenson fell asleep on the floor of the compound. Two hours later he was rudely awakened by someone dangling a kerosene lantern in front of his face,

> sending shadows lurching grotesquely up the walls. Behind the lamp, Mortenson saw the barrel of an AK-47 aimed, he realized, his consciousness ratcheting up a notch with this information, at his chest. Behind the gun, a wild man with a matted beard and gray turban was shouting in a language he didn't understand.

Mortenson was jerked to his feet and dragged out the door, where he was blindfolded, thrown in the bed of a pickup truck, and driven to another location. There, he was locked inside a "spare, high-ceilinged room" with a "single small window, shuttered from outside," and guarded by two thugs with AK-47s. In the morning, when Mortenson indicated he needed to visit a toilet, his abductors escorted him to a crude stall with a squat latrine, where one of the guards "walked inside with him while the other stared in from outside." Mortenson explained, "To have to, you know, clean yourself afterward while they stare at you, was nerve-wracking."

According to Mortenson, he was imprisoned for eight days, with nothing to read but "a tattered *Time* magazine dated November 1979." By the middle of his fifth night in captivity,

> Mortenson felt a wave of blackness lapping at his feet, surging up to his knees, threatening to drown him in despair.... Through force of will, Mortenson held the black water at bay, and turned the pages of the magazine, searching for a foothold in the warm dry world he'd left behind. Dawn of his sixth morning in captivity found Mortenson's eyes tearing up over an ad for a WaterPik Oral Hygiene Appliance.

By and by, the ringleader who ordered his abduction showed up, a man described by Mortenson as "an emerging Taliban commander" who spoke perfect English. Mortenson told the commander he ran a charity that was building a school in Baltistan, and "planned to build many more schools for Pakistan's most neglected children," hoping his good intentions would convince the Talib to release him, but the gambit failed. So Mortenson tried a different tack, telling the commander that his wife was about to give birth to their first child, a son (even though Mortenson had already learned that the baby would be a daughter), because he "knew that for a Muslim the birth of a son is a really big deal.... I felt bad about lying, but I thought the birth of a son might make them let me go."

This ploy, alas, also failed to win his freedom. At 4:00 in the morning of the ninth day, when the commander blindfolded Mortenson and put him in the bed of a pickup truck full of armed men, Mortenson assumed his execution was imminent:

> Back then, before 9/11, beheading foreigners wasn't in fashion.... And I didn't think being shot was such a bad way to die. But the idea that Tara would have to raise our child on her own and would probably never find out what happened to me made me crazy. I could picture her pain and uncertainty going on and on and that seemed like the most horrible thing of all.

Fortunately, as Mortenson was taking what he feared were his final breaths, the truck skidded to a stop, whereupon the commander removed Mortenson's blindfold and gave him a hug. "We're throwing a party," the Talib announced. "A party before we take you back to Peshawar." Instead of being executed by a Taliban firing squad, Mortenson was feted as the guest of honor at a rowdy Pashtun hoedown featuring barbecued goat, lots of hashish, and boisterous dancing. Throughout the bacchanal, dozens of Taliban embraced Mortenson like a long-lost brother and stuffed wads of hundred-rupee notes into his pockets. "For your schools!" the commander explained, shouting in Mortenson's ear to be heard over bursts of celebratory gunfire. "So, *Inshallah*, you'll build many more!"

> Giddily [Mortenson] joined the celebration, goat grease trickling down his eight-day beard, performing the old Tanzanian steps he thought he'd forgotten to shouts of encouragement from the Wazir, dancing with the absolute bliss, with the wild abandon, bequeathed by freedom.

If this stirring resolution to Mortenson's ordeal seems a bit far-fetched, it is. The entire story was fabricated. There was no wild party, no Taliban commander, no abduction of any sort. According to Mansur Khan Mahsud, a Pakistani scholar who frequently accompanied Mortenson during his visit to Tehsil Ladha, Mortenson was never threatened, no one ever pointed a gun at him, and no one ever held him against his will, even momentarily, during the approximately fifteen days he spent in South Waziristan. "Greg was never worried or frightened," says Mansur Khan, now the director of Research and Administration at the FATA Research Centre, an internationally respected, nonpartisan think tank in Islamabad. "No, no, no. He really enjoyed his stay there. And he was given very good treatment. If he tells, 'I have been kidnapped,' he is lying. He was an honored guest of the whole village."

According to Peter Bergen, a national security analyst for the CNN television network,

> Mansur Khan...is somebody I've worked with, and he's actually done academic papers for the foundation that I work at. He's a well-known academic in the region. The idea that he's a member of the Taliban who kidnapped Greg Mortenson is just absurd.

During Mortenson's visit to Ladha, he was housed in a village called Kot Langerkhel, at the home of the deputy inspector general of the police. A photograph shows Mortenson relaxing in this home, which had comfortable furniture and was connected to the national electrical grid. According to Mortenson, he was abducted in the middle of his first night in South Waziristan, and spent every night thereafter in captivity sleeping on an earthen floor "under a musty blanket." But the photo shows Mortenson smiling broadly as he sits on the deputy inspector general's Western-style bed, replete with a mattress and clean linens.

In another photograph, Mortenson is strolling across a field above Kot Langerkhel on a lovely July afternoon, accompanied by Naimat Gul Mahsud, Naimat Gul's young nephew, and his servant. A handwritten note from Sangi Marjan, the commissioner of education, attests to a pleasant visit with Mortenson during the period Mortenson claims to have been held captive. According to Mansur Khan, Mortenson was introduced to everyone he met as "a professor at an American medical college." Villagers came from throughout Ladha to

Greg Mortenson (standing, center, holding an AK-47 rifle) with some of the men he would falsely accuse of having kidnapped him for eight days in July 1996. Mansur Khan Mahsud is on the far right.

receive treatment from him, and he became quite a popular figure.

It is nearly impossible to overstate the importance of personal reputation to Pashtuns in general, and members of the Mahsud tribe in particular. Upholding one's honor, and the honor of one's clan, is the preeminent tenet of *Pashtunwali*, the overarching moral code that has shaped Mahsud culture and identity for centuries. By offering to act as Mortenson's host and guardian in South Waziristan, Naimat Gul obligated his branch of the Mahsud tribe to protect Mortenson from physical injury and personal affront. The village of Kot Langerkhel took this responsibility quite seriously. Mahsud tribesmen, armed with Kalashnikov automatic rifles, volunteered to accompany Mortenson whenever he traveled beyond the center of the village. "I myself accompanied Greg two or three times during his visit to different areas in South Waziristan Agency," says Mansur Khan, who was twenty-five years old at the time.

In *Stones into Schools*—Mortenson's second book, pub-

COURTESY OF: NAIMAT GUL MAHSUD

"Instead of telling the world about our frustration, deprivation, illiteracy, and tradition of hospitality," says Naimut Gul Mahsud (with Mortenson en route to the alleged kidnapping in 1996), "he invented a false story...."

lished in 2009—there is a color photograph of thirteen men holding Kalashnikovs. The caption identifies them as "Waziri tribesmen who abducted Greg Mortenson near Razmak, North Waziristan. Greg was detained there for eight days in July 1996." But according to Mansur Khan, who is one of the individuals depicted, all the men in the photo are members of the Mahsud tribe, not Wazirs (who are sworn enemies of the Mahsuds), and they were Mortenson's guardians, not his abductors. "This picture was taken in Ladha, not in Razmak, North Waziristan Agency," Mansur Khan scoffs. "This was a leisure trip to show Greg different places in Ladha." Unpublished photographs taken at the same time and place, date-stamped "7-21-96," show Mortenson clutching an AK-47 and wearing a rack of ammunition across his chest, hamming it up beside Mansur Khan and other Mahsud tribesmen who volunteered to serve as Mortenson's bodyguards—most of whom appear in the *Stones into Schools* photo as well.

A preponderance of evidence indicates that Mortenson

manufactured his account of being kidnapped by the Taliban out of whole cloth, apparently for the same reason he's invented so many other anecdotes of personal derring-do in his books and public appearances: to inflate the myth of Greg Mortenson, "the astonishing, uplifting story of a real-life Indiana Jones and his remarkable humanitarian campaign in the Taliban's backyard," as the back cover of *Three Cups of Tea* puts it. The likelihood that anyone in the United States would ever discover the truth about what happened in an exceedingly isolated Pakistani village must have seemed infinitesimal to Mortenson.

The truth, says Mansur Khan Mahsud, is that "in 1996 there were no Taliban operating anywhere near Ladha. The Taliban didn't come until 2001." Although a ruthless faction known as the Tehrik-i-Taliban now holds sway over much of South Waziristan, Mansur Khan points out that it was only after the U.S. invasion of Afghanistan, post–9/11, that large numbers of Taliban fled across the Durand Line into the tribal areas of Pakistan, seeking refuge from American drones and bombers.

The fact is, almost every person Mortenson encountered during his visit to Ladha treated him graciously. Only once was Mortenson made to feel less than completely welcome: Near the end of July, the South Waziristan Political Agent heard that a foreigner was vacationing in Kot Langerkhel, prompting government authorities to ask Naimat Gul Mahsud to escort Mortenson out of the banned tribal areas as soon as possible. A few days later, Naimat Gul drove Mortenson to Peshawar International Airport and put him on a plane for Islamabad.

When the residents of Ladha bid goodbye to Mortenson, they did so with affection, and they believed the feeling was mutual. "Years later," says Naimat Gul, "when I scanned through the book *Three Cups of Tea* and read that Greg had been abducted and threatened with guns, I was shocked. Instead of telling the world about our frustration, deprivation, illiteracy, and tradition of hospitality, he invented a false story about being abducted by savages. I do not understand why he did this."[2]

· Part II ·
PENNIES FOR PEACE, MILLIONS FOR MORTENSON

"[T]he duties of speaking, promoting, and fund-raising into which I have been thrust... have often made me feel like a man caught in the act of conducting an illicit affair with the dark side of his own personality."

—GREG MORTENSON,
STONES INTO SCHOOLS

IN THE FALL OF 1993, when Mortenson arrived home from K2, he immediately started soliciting donations for his "Khane school project." A year later, he had managed to raise just $723. "If it hadn't been for Jean," muses Jennifer Wilson, referring to Jean Hoerni, her late husband, "Greg would still be a nurse." In September 1994, Hoerni gave Mortenson the $12,000 he needed to build his first school, thereby launching his career as a humanitarian. Hoerni was a brilliant theoretical physicist who in the late 1950s played a pivotal role in the invention of the planar transistor, a new type of semiconductor that enabled the mass production of silicon chips—thereby transforming not only the electronics industry but also life as we know it. According to Stanford University historian Michael Riordan, "Hoerni's elegant idea helped to establish Silicon Valley as the microelectronics epicenter of the world." It also made Hoerni a wealthy man.

Hoerni had moved to California in 1952 at the age of twenty-eight, but he was born and raised in Switzerland, where he had developed a lifelong passion for mountains and mountaineering. Around 1990, Hoerni met Jennifer Wilson, their friendship gradually evolved into something more serious, and in the summer of 1993 he invited her on a twenty-eight-day, two-hundred-mile trek through the Himalaya, in the northern Indian regions of Zanskar and Ladakh. "I had never even been camping before," says Wilson, a businesswoman who grew up in Iowa. "It was a completely new experience for me. It was amazing." Four months after returning from India, Wilson and Hoerni got married. He was sixty-nine; she was forty-five.

In the fall of 1994, Hoerni happened to read Mortenson's article in the American Himalayan Foundation newsletter about his quixotic scheme to build a school in Baltistan. Having trekked up the Baltoro Glacier to K2 on two occasions, Hoerni was familiar with the region, and the venture piqued his imagination. "I was in the kitchen," Wilson remembers. "Jean came in and said, 'Look at this article about this guy who is trying to build a school. Americans don't care about Muslims; they only care about Buddhist Sherpas in Nepal.

No one is going to contribute to this. I'm going to call this guy.'" Hoerni, who was living in Seattle, had a brief phone conversation with Mortenson, and then wrote him a $12,000 check. After the call, Wilson recalls, "Jean actually said, 'This guy may just take off with my money. But I'm going to take a chance on him.' It was really an act of faith." As soon as the check cleared the bank, Mortenson departed for Pakistan to build his first school.

In December 1996, when Mortenson reported to Hoerni that the school was finally finished, Hoerni didn't care that it had been built in Korphe instead of Khane; he was simply happy that it had been completed while he was still around to hear about it. Eighteen months earlier, he and Wilson had been hiking up a mountain in the Swiss Jura, Wilson says, "and Jean couldn't keep up with me. That was unprecedented." Although Hoerni was seventy at the time, up until that moment he had been as strong as a man many years his junior; the previous summer he had trekked over an 18,400-foot Tibetan pass at a blistering pace. Concerned about his persistent, uncharacteristic fatigue, Wilson persuaded Hoerni to make an appointment to see his brother, Marc, who was a doctor in Geneva. A blood test revealed that Jean had acute leukemia. He was expected to die within a few months.

Nevertheless, for about a year after his diagnosis, Hoerni managed to remain active. "We weren't able to hike as vigorously," says Wilson, "but he was still able to hike. The doctors were kind of astonished." In July 1996, however, while Mortenson was sojourning in South Waziristan, Hoerni underwent emergency surgery to remove his spleen. He nearly died on the operating table. Upon his release from the hospital, his skin remained ashen and he grew increasingly frail.

Back in 1995, nearly a year after Hoerni had given Mortenson the $12,000 he needed to start working in Pakistan, he paid for Mortenson to fly to Seattle so they could meet face to face. "They bonded immediately," says Wilson. Hoerni admired Mortenson's chutzpah, his willingness to think big. Both men loved the mountains. Both were visionaries, rule breakers, and risk takers—perennial outsiders who had scant regard for societal conventions.

Hoerni treated Mortenson like a son, and his affection was reciprocated, according to Wilson: "Greg told me that Jean became kind of a father figure to him, perhaps because his own father had died." In the wake of their Seattle rendezvous, Hoerni was so enamored of Mortenson and his humanitarian goals that he gave him $250,000 to build five more schools in Pakistan, even though the Korphe project had barely gotten off the ground. In order to make this donation tax-deductible, Hoerni channeled it to Mortenson through a special account at the American Himalayan Foundation, designated the Hoerni/Pakistan Fund. Then, just a year later in the autumn of 1996, when it became obvious to Hoerni that his death was imminent, he established a stand-alone, tax-exempt charity for Mortenson, endowing it with an additional million dollars. Thus did the Central Asia Institute come into existence.

As 1996 drew to a close and Hoerni's decline accelerated, Mortenson flew to Seattle to spend a few days with his benefactor before the end. During this farewell visit, Mortenson made good use of his nursing skills to make Hoerni as comfortable as possible, and Hoerni seemed grateful for his presence. On January 12, 1997, not long after Mortenson returned to Montana, Jean Hoerni died, with his wife and daughters at his bedside.

★ ★ ★

ONE OF MORTENSON'S childhood heroes was Mother Teresa. According to *Three Cups of Tea* (page 236), Mortenson "admired her determination to serve the world's most neglected populations." A hospice for the terminally ill that she opened in Dar es Salaam, Tanzania, in 1968 captured Greg's imagination as a ten-year-old growing up in the village of Moshi, 275 miles to the north, and his respect for Mother Teresa became greater still when she was awarded the Nobel Peace Prize in 1979. Mortenson came to regard her as a role model, even after she faced withering criticism over the shoddy medical care her hospices provided and for lying to donors about how their contributions were used. According to *Three Cups,*

> Mortenson had heard the criticism of the woman.... He'd read her defense of her practice of taking donations from unsavory sources, like drug dealers, corporate criminals, and corrupt politicians hoping to purchase their own path to salvation. After his own struggle to raise funds for the children of Pakistan, he felt he understood what had driven her to famously dismiss her critics by saying, "I don't care where the money comes from. It's all washed clean in the service of God."

Mortenson's 1993 trip to K2 had ignited in him a powerful ambition to improve the lives of villagers in the mountains of northeastern Pakistan, an ambition inspired in part by Mother Teresa. Hoerni's generosity granted Mortenson an extraordinary opportunity to realize this dream. By the end of 2000, he had built more than twenty schools, with dozens more in the pipeline, an impressive feat by any measure. In September of that year, during a layover at Calcutta International Airport while flying home from a trip to observe and learn from successful NGOs in Bangladesh, according to *Three Cups of Tea* (pages 235–237), "Mortenson learned that one of his heroes, Mother Teresa, had died after a long illness . . . and decided to try and pay her his respects." Arriving at the Missionaries of Charity Mother House after the front gate was locked for the evening, he was admitted by a nun and escorted down a dark hallway to view Mother Teresa's corpse:

> She lay on a simple cot, at the center of a bright room full of flickering devotional candles. Mortenson gently nudged other bouquets aside, making room for his gaudy offering, and took a seat against a wall. The nun, backing out the door, left him alone with Mother Teresa. . . .
> "I sat in the corner staring at this shrouded figure," Mortenson says. "She looked so small, draped in her cloth.

And I remember thinking how amazing it was that such a tiny person had such a huge effect on humanity.". . . .

Nuns, visiting the room to pay their respects, had knelt to touch Mother Teresa's feet. He could see where the cream-colored muslin had been discolored from the laying on of hundreds of hands. But it didn't feel right to touch her feet. Mortenson knelt on the cool tiled floor next to Mother Teresa and placed his large palm over her small hand. It covered it completely. . . .

Safely back in his basement, during the winter of 2000, Mortenson often reflected on those few rare moments with Mother Teresa.

This account of Mortenson's pilgrimage to visit the mortal remains of the woman who inspired his life work is poignant and beautiful. But it's difficult to reconcile with the fact that Mother Teresa died on September 5, 1997, three years before Mortenson says he knelt beside her in Calcutta.

★ ★ ★

"WE CAN CONSTRUCT and maintain a school for a generation that will educate thousands of children for less than $20,000," he asserted in interviews and public presentations. But in truth, CAI was spending $50,000 or more—sometimes a lot more—just to build a single school, and the funds coming in were significantly less than the funds going out. Four years after Hoerni's death, Mortenson had already burned through most of Hoerni's money, and CAI teetered on the brink of insolvency.

"Greg had no sense of what it takes to run a business," says Jennifer Wilson, who joined CAI's board of directors shortly after Hoerni passed away. "Jean was able to make Greg do things and hold him accountable, but after Jean was gone, Greg wouldn't answer to anyone.... Tom Vaughan was a sweetheart, but Greg could always find his way around him."

Vaughan, a genial San Francisco pulmonologist and mountaineer who died in 2009, served as chairman of the

CAI board. "Even when he was home, we often wouldn't hear from Greg for weeks," Vaughan laments in *Three Cups of Tea,* in one of the rare criticisms of Mortenson that appears in the book. "And he wouldn't return phone calls or emails. The board had a discussion about trying to make Greg account for how he spent his time, but we realized that would never work. Greg just does whatever he wants." Most of the directors, like Vaughan, were frustrated by Mortenson's passive-aggressive disposition, and his disdain for routine business practices.

In late 1999, with Mortenson's encouragement, Tom Hornbein was asked to join CAI's board to boost fundraising and provide the organization with some badly needed discipline. Thirty-six years earlier, Hornbein had made the first ascent of the formidable West Ridge of Mount Everest, still widely considered one of the greatest accomplishments in mountaineering history. President John F. Kennedy awarded the Hubbard Medal to Hornbein and his Everest teammates (one of whom was Mortenson's future father-in-law, Barry Bishop). In a distinguished career after Everest, Hornbein served as chairman of the anesthesiology department at the University of Washington School of Medicine, where he earned a reputation as a demanding but compassionate *jefe*.

"Tom Hornbein was really fun to work with," Jennifer Wilson remembers of their years together on the CAI board. "He and I agreed on so many levels, especially about the need to hold Greg accountable and somehow get him to be more businesslike."

But the harder Hornbein, Wilson, and other CAI directors tried to persuade Mortenson to heed their edicts about providing receipts, documenting expenses, and conforming to IRS regulations, the more intransigent he became. By 2001, when Hornbein succeeded Tom Vaughan as chairman of the CAI board, relations between Mortenson and the rest of the board were nearing the flash point. In an email to Mortenson dated September 20, 2001, Hornbein warned,

> I write to share with you my continuing concerns about our relationship in our roles as Director and Board chair.... The

underlying issues are ones of communication between the two of us, and trust.... Whatever the stigma, if you and I are not able to work out a more facile, productive communication, I doubt my ability to fulfill my responsibility to you and the CAI Board.... We exist, whether you consider us a pain-in-the-ass at times or not. Unless you would wish to and are capable of being a one man show (as it was in the beginning), then you are stuck with and need us.

When he sent this email, Hornbein was feverishly organizing a major fundraiser for CAI, to be held twelve days hence at Seattle's Town Hall, and he asked me to serve as Mortenson's opening act. I'd met Greg four or five times by then, and I was enormously impressed by what he'd done in Pakistan. When Greg explained to me that it had all begun with a promise he'd made to the people of Korphe in 1993, after he'd accidentally wandered into their village and they'd nursed him back to health, I was profoundly moved. Over the previous three years I'd donated more than $55,000 to CAI, and I'd committed to donating another $20,000 in 2002. I told Hornbein I would be honored to introduce Greg at the fundraiser.

The event did not begin well. Mortenson arrived an hour late. When Hornbein admonished him for keeping the packed house waiting, Greg sulked and threatened to fly home without speaking. Only after much inveigling did Greg eventually consent to go on stage. When things finally got under way, I concluded my introduction by telling the audience, "What Greg has accomplished, with very little money, verges on the miraculous." As he shambled up to the podium and gave me a hug, the auditorium filled with thunderous applause. Greg's presentation knocked the crowd's socks off, and the fundraiser turned out to be a notable success.

Relations between Mortenson and the CAI board, however, continued to deteriorate. "I would talk to people who expressed interest in making a sizable contribution," says Jennifer Wilson, "but when they tried to contact Greg he wouldn't get back to them. Other people who actually made big contributions never got follow-ups from Greg. We kept trying to persuade Greg to hire an administrator who would do all the stuff he wasn't good at, but he refused.... At the time, I didn't understand. Now that I know about the things he was hiding, I realize he didn't want anyone looking over his shoulder. That would have been tremendously threatening to him."

By early 2002, Mortenson pretty much stopped communicating with the board altogether. Exasperated, Wilson quit. At the conclusion of a contentious board meeting on September 7, 2002, Hornbein and two other hard-working directors, Gordon Wiltsie and Sally Uhlmann, left the board as well. In a letter to the other directors explaining his resignation, Hornbein wrote,

> I am devastated by what has happened.... While my belief in CAI's mission is undiminished, I can no longer believe that Greg, in spite of his unswerving commitment, has the attributes demanded to lead CAI into its next phase.... Communication is essential to trust. Accountability with transparency underpins trust.... Many of the Board's efforts to achieve this accountability have been thwarted by Greg, simply by his not responding. It was Greg's vision and courage that created CAI and caused us to commit our energies. He is a unique individual with many precious attributes. Now, sadly, it is other aspects of Greg, ones I don't understand, that leave me doubting the future viability of his dream.

For his part, Mortenson was elated by the departure of Wilson, Hornbein, Wiltsie, and Uhlmann, and simply swept the issues they'd raised under the rug. His stonewalling had achieved its desired end, leaving him essentially unaccountable to anyone. In an email to CAI board members and staffers, Mortenson disingenuously gushed,

> I want to express my personal gratitude and thanks to Tom Hornbein, Sally and Gordon for their tremendous effort as Board Directors. Your assistance was a catalyst at a crucial time in CAI's evolution. From the bottom of my heart, thank

you. I would also like to extend a belated thanks to Jennifer Wilson for your many years of support that provided continuity and stability from the inception of our efforts.... Despite unrest and uncertainty, this past year has been CAI's most successful year ever in Pakistan.... Onward ho.

Despite this public effusion of gratitude, in private Mortenson told anyone who would listen that Hornbein's criticisms of him were motivated by self-regard and envy. Hornbein, Greg explained, simply wanted to take control of CAI in order to create a legacy for himself. Other board members who witnessed Hornbein and Mortenson interacting during this period have dismissed Mortenson's interpretation as preposterous.

Dealing with Mortenson's idiosyncrasies was stressful for the entire board. Nonetheless, Jennifer Wilson insists, "No matter how many problems I had working with Greg, I never, ever thought of him as evil. And believe me, I've had opportunities where I could have felt that way." It's hard for her to be angry with Mortenson, she says, because "he isn't a normal person. It's almost like he's from another planet.... For years, he struggled to find a place in our Western culture. Then, thanks to Jean's money, Greg figured out how to be extraordinarily successful working in a very different culture." She believes it would be an exercise in futility to expect Mortenson ever to conform to Western norms of doing business—or anything else.

★　★　★

MORTENSON'S BULLISH PRONOUNCEMENT to the CAI board notwithstanding, at the end of 2002 "the organization's finances were as shaky as ever," *Three Cups of Tea* reports on page 295. "So Mortenson decided to defer the raise the board had approved for him, from twenty-eight thousand dollars to thirty-five thousand dollars a year."

Although the first statement (about CAI's shaky finances) is true, the latter statement is not. According to

CAI financial records, Mortenson's CAI salary for 2002 was $41,200, plus $12,087 in employee benefits and deferred compensation; in 2003 his salary increased to $47,197, plus $6,547 in benefits. Furthermore, since 1995, he had been quietly drawing a stipend amounting to $21,792 per year from the AHF Hoerni/Pakistan Fund in addition to his CAI salary package.[3] All told, at the time Mortenson claimed he was being paid $28,000, his annual compensation actually exceeded $75,000. One could make a strong case that Mortenson deserved every penny of it, given how hard he worked and what a crucial role he played in all aspects of CAI's operation. What's disturbing is not the amount Mortenson was paid, but that he lied about it—and that dozens of such falsehoods are strewn throughout the book.

In any case, by the fall of 2003, CAI's financial difficulties had ended. On April 6 of that year, Mortenson appeared on the cover of *Parade* magazine. Inside, an article titled "He Fights Terror With Books" described how Greg found himself in Korphe after retreating from K2 in 1993. After the Korphe villagers nursed him back to health, Mortenson repaid their kindness by building them a school, and in the years that followed he constructed dozens of other schools in northern Pakistan and neighboring Afghanistan. These schools, the article explained, helped to counter the influence of fundamentalist *madrassas*:

> "In the past 10 years," says Mortenson, "more than 80,000 Pakistani and Afghani boys who received hard-line religious instruction in these *madrassas* were fed directly into the ranks of the Taliban. Islamic extremists know they can use these religious schools as an effective vehicle for recruiting terrorists. The West has so far failed to recognize that offering an alternative by building secular schools is the cheapest and most effective way of combating terrorism."

Thirty-four million copies of the magazine were distributed across the country. The article included a mailing address, an email address, and a toll-free number for Central

Asia Institute. Before publication, Mortenson had hired extra staff and set up a phone bank to answer calls to handle the anticipated response. Within a few days, says one of those new employees, "We needed a wheelbarrow for all the mailbags stuffed with checks arriving at the office." By the end of 2003, the organization had received more than a million dollars in donations. The CAI board of directors (which by then consisted of Mortenson and three loyal admirers) raised Mortenson's annual salary to $112,000, and Mortenson announced an ambitious plan to use the *Parade* donations to expand CAI's programs in Afghanistan.

In the autumn of 2003, Mortenson flew to Afghanistan with funds to construct half a dozen schools in the least-developed corner of that nation, the mysterious Wakhan Corridor. According to *Three Cups of Tea* (pages 314–316), Mortenson enjoyed a long conversation with the king of Afghanistan during this trip, aboard a Pakistan International Airlines flight to Kabul:

> The king sat in the window seat. Mortenson recognized him from pictures on the old Afghan currency he'd seen for sale in the bazaars. At eighty-nine, Zahir Shah looked far older than his official portrait as he stared out the window of the PIA 737 at the country he'd been exiled from for nearly thirty years.
>
> Aside from the king's security detail and a small crew of stewardesses, Mortenson was alone on the short flight from Islamabad to Kabul with Afghanistan's former monarch. When Shah turned away from the window, he locked eyes with Mortenson across the aisle.
>
> *"As-Salaam Alaaikum*, sir," Mortenson said.
>
> "And to you, sir," Shah replied.

When Mortenson told the king that he was en route to northern Afghanistan's seldom-visited Wakhan region to build schools, Zaher Shah patted the empty seat beside him and invited Greg to sit there. For the remainder of the flight they discussed the remoteness of the Wakhan, the recent invasion of Iraq, and how the latter was diverting crucial American resources and personnel from Afghanistan.

> Zahir Shah placed his hand, with its enormous lapis ring, on Mortenson's. "I'm glad one American is here at least," he said. "The man you want to see up north is Sadhar Khan. He's a *mujahid*. But he cares about his people."
> "So I've heard," Mortenson said.
> Zahir Shah pulled a calling card out of the breast pocket of the business suit he wore under his striped robe and called for one of his security guards to bring his valise. Then the king held his thumb to an inkpad and pressed his print on the back of the card. "It may be helpful if you give this to *Commandhan* Khan," he said. "Allah be with you. And go with my blessing."

It's a memorable account, layered with vivid particulars. It also happens to be fictitious. His Majesty Zaher Shah died in 2007, but when I contacted a close associate of the king to verify Mortenson's story, he forwarded my query to Mostapha Zaher, the monarch's grandson and successor. Zaher's reply was immediate and unequivocal:

> I wish to categorically state, and in no uncertain terms, that my late grandfather had NEVER taken the mentioned flight PIA 737 from Islamabad to Kabul during the Holy Month Ramadhan of 2003. As a matter of fact, he has NEVER traveled on any PIA flights from 1973 to 2007, the year of his passing away [emphasis by Zaher]. The information provided by the person [Mortenson] is simply not factual.

★ ★ ★

IN THE WAKE of the *Parade* article, as Mortenson's fame continued to grow and the donations kept increasing, his grandiosity and mendacity only became more pronounced. "Greg was horrible to work for," says an ex-employee whom Mortenson hired when the CAI staff expanded to make the most of the *Parade* donations.

"It was very important for him to test people, to test their loyalty," explains another staffer who was brought on around the same time. "He played a lot of mind games. His management style was to divide and conquer. He'd lean forward, tell you how important you were to him, then badmouth other staff so you felt like he was confiding in you. But the staff talked to each other, so we learned he was badmouthing each of us to everyone else. We were all like, 'You're kidding! That's what he told you?'

"Working for Greg was like being on a roller coaster," this ex-employee continues. "One day he was telling you how great you were, and then for no apparent reason he would give you the icy treatment.... We went through a two- or three-month period where Greg wasn't communicating with the staff at all."

Three Cups of Tea never mentions this aspect of Mortenson's personality, although it frequently refers to his chronic tardiness. David Relin, Mortenson's co-author, writes in the introduction, "During the two years we worked together on this book, Mortenson was often so maddeningly late for appointments that I considered abandoning the project." On page 39, Mortenson's mother says, "Greg has never been on time in his life.... Ever since he was a boy, Greg has always operated on African time." In 1998, Mortenson showed up three weeks late for a rendezvous in China with his friend Scott Darsney, who was kept waiting in Beijing until Greg finally appeared. Mortenson's aversion to punctuality is presented in *Three Cups of Tea* as if it were an endearing quirk. To a number of people who worked with Mortenson over the years, however, his habitual lateness—like his habitual lying—seemed more pathological than quirky.

★   ★   ★

UNTIL RECENTLY, I didn't know that the most dramatic anecdotes in *Three Cups of Tea* were fabricated, but by 2004 I had begun to suspect that Mortenson was improperly using CAI funds. After Tom Hornbein, Sally Uhlmann, and

Gordon Wiltsie resigned from the CAI board of directors, I asked Wiltsie, who had served as the board treasurer, why he left. "Greg," he replied, "regards CAI as his personal ATM." Wiltsie described how Mortenson would routinely charge personal expenses to CAI, and seldom provided receipts or other documentation for any of his expenditures, no matter how persistently Wiltsie pleaded with him to do so.

At that point, I had donated more than $75,000 to CAI. On March 23, 2004, I sent a fax to Mortenson's office:

> I have decided to suspend my financial support of CAI for the indefinite future. I didn't make this decision lightly. After interviewing several of the people who recently left the board of directors I lost confidence in Greg's accountability. I feel that I cannot continue to give such large sums of money (they seem large to me, at any rate) to an organization run with so little oversight and such lax accounting practices. It is possible that I may decide to support CAI again at some future date. But not until CAI has installed a strong, active board of directors who keep close tabs on how the organization is run. Make no mistake: I still believe in CAI's mission, but I am made extremely uneasy by Greg's way of running the show. Although I don't want to make any public statements that would have a negative impact on Greg's work, I no longer feel comfortable providing financial backing, or lending my name, to CAI.

Debbie Raynor, CAI's chief financial officer at the time, remembers this missive well, because it matched her own experiences with Mortenson so precisely. When my letter rattled out of the CAI fax machine, she had been trying, unsuccessfully, to persuade Mortenson to document his expenses for the previous eight months. She had come on board as CFO in July 2003, and her duties soon expanded to include staff supervisor and board treasurer. By the summer of 2004, however, Mortenson's conduct made it impossible for Raynor to continue working for CAI in good conscience. As she explained in a memo to the CAI board of directors, there were no meaningful financial policies or procedures in place when I started my employment. I endeavored to rectify that situation and bring about necessary and much needed financial controls.... These new policies were fully discussed and implemented with full approval by Mr. Mortenson. The staff readily complied with these new policies ensuring an accurate account of expenses. However, Mr. Mortenson has failed to comply in any meaningful manner with these policies.... Since the start of my employment, Mr. Mortenson has spent over $100,000 on CAI's credit cards. Mr. Mortenson has never provided any receipts for these expenses, and repeatedly ignored my requests for their submission.... Mr. Mortenson has refused to submit even one travel voucher.... In order to allocate indirect expenses, it is imperative that I receive time sheets from all employees. Since March 2004, Mr. Mortenson has failed to submit a time sheet.

On May 27, 2004, I again reported to the Board the serious situation as it related to overseas expenses. At that time, there was over $100,000 in unaccounted overseas expenses. Mr. Mortenson agreed to provide all documentation for overseas expenses. To date, he has not produced the promised documents in any meaningful manner. In fact, currently CAI has spent over **$270,000 in cash and wire transfers** [emphasis by Raynor] without proper documentation as to the disbursement of this money. There is no record to who ultimately received these monies or the manner in which it was spent.

Mr. Mortenson has reported that measures have been implemented to resolve the unsubstantiated overseas documentation; however, no specifics have been forthcoming.

In August 2004, I learned that information given to me to be placed in the Annual Report is untrue and therefore fraudulent.

Unfortunately, Mr. Mortenson has determined that he has no need of providing financial information to the CFO. These circumstances are untenable. I am unable to fulfill the duties and responsibilities as CFO and Staff Supervisor. Thus, I had no alternative but to resign from CAI effective September 3, 2004.

★ ★ ★

IN MARCH 2006, Viking Penguin published *Three Cups of Tea* in hardcover. Later that year, the CAI board of directors increased Mortenson's annual salary to $145,000. When the paperback edition of *Three Cups of Tea* came out in January 2007, the book vaulted to the top of the *New York Times* paperback nonfiction bestseller list and remained at number one for forty-three weeks. To capitalize on the resulting publicity, as Mortenson would later explain in *Stones into Schools*, he resolved to turn CAI "into a promotion-and-fundraising machine" by launching what amounted to a perpetual book tour—an exhausting schedule of public appearances that continued until Mortenson's misconduct was revealed in April 2011. This relentless marketing campaign reaped impressive rewards. In 2006, CAI's total revenue amounted to $1.6 million. In 2007 it was $3.8 million. In 2008, it ballooned to $14.1 million, $14.3 million in 2009, and $22.7 million in 2010.

Mortenson has not been shy about taking credit for the windfall CAI has received from his promotional efforts. He has been more reticent about acknowledging the millions of dollars that have flowed into his personal bank account along the way. It may surprise many people who have donated money to CAI, as it surprised me, to learn that CAI received none of the proceeds from any of Mortenson's books until *60 Minutes* brought this fact to light in 2011. All of the royalties from *Three Cups of Tea* were split equally by Mortenson and David Relin. All of the royalties from his other books were paid to Mortenson alone.

CAI supporters may be even more dismayed to learn, as I was, that although CAI received no royalties from Mortenson's books, CAI paid virtually all of the expenses incurred by Mortenson, Relin, and at least some of his uncredited ghostwriters while they were researching, writing, and promoting the books. These expenses included cameras, computers, writers' advances, and travel. When Mortenson traveled domestically to promote his books in recent years, he usually flew on chartered jets, and CAI paid millions of dollars for these charters. CAI also paid millions of dollars to run numerous ads to promote Mortenson's books in upscale publications such as *The New Yorker, The Atlantic, Harper's,* and *The New York Times.*

Following the publication of *Three Cups of Tea*, Mortenson made hundreds of appearances to talk about CAI and his books. As Mortenson writes in *Stones into Schools,*

> each time I travel somewhere new, I am still shocked by the sheer number of people who flock to hear this tale. Last summer in Boston...the organizers of a talk I was giving at Northeastern University...booked me into a hockey stadium and filled the place with 5,600 people. A week later at a basketball arena in Murfreesboro, Tennessee, 9,500 folks showed up and my speech had to be broadcast on a JumboTron.

Using CAI funds, Mortenson has purchased hundreds of thousands of copies of *Three Cups of Tea* and *Stones into Schools*, which he has subsequently handed out to attendees at his speaking engagements. A significant number of these books were charged to CAI's Pennies for Peace program, contrary to Mortenson's frequent assertions that CAI uses "every penny" of every donation made to Pennies for Peace to support schools in Pakistan and Afghanistan. Rather than buy Mortenson's books at wholesale cost from his publisher, moreover, CAI has paid retail price from commercial outlets such as Borders, Barnes & Noble, and Amazon. Buying from retailers allowed Mortenson to receive his author's royalty for each book given away, and also allowed these handouts to augment his ranking on national bestseller lists. (Had he ordered the books from his publisher, Mortenson would not have received a royalty, nor would bestseller lists have reflected those purchases.) According to one of Mortenson's friends, when he learned that Elizabeth Gilbert's *Eat, Pray, Love* had bumped *Three Cups of Tea* from number one down to number two on the *New York Times* paperback nonfiction list, "Greg was furious. He started buying books like crazy, with the CAI credit card, to try and put *Three Cups* back on top."

Book sales aside, Mortenson's speaking engagements—which are arranged by the Penguin Speakers Bureau, a division of the corporation that publishes his books, Penguin Group USA—were extremely lucrative for him. When Mortenson traveled to speak, he typically did two or three events per city. He appeared at many of them pro bono, but for some sixty events each year he charged upwards of $30,000 per event, plus $3,000 in travel expenses—despite the fact that CAI, not Mortenson, has paid for all of his travel costs (including chartered jets and deluxe hotel suites), as well as expenses incurred by family members and personal assistants who often traveled with him. "Greg is of the attitude that CAI exists because of him," says an ex-staffer who held a senior position in the organization's Montana office. "Any money he raises for CAI, according to Greg's logic, is therefore his money, and he can spend it however he wants."

Until recently, the CAI website stated, "Central Asia Institute is a non-profit 501(c)3 organization dedicated to use every dollar contributed as efficiently as possible. It is our goal to spend no more than 15% of your donation on overhead (administrative and fundraising costs), and to spend 85% of your contribution on our programs." What this statement failed to disclose is that for accounting purposes, CAI reported the millions of dollars it spent on book advertising and chartered jets as "program expenses," rather than as fundraising or other overhead. Were they reported honestly, CAI's fundraising and administrative expenses would actually have exceeded 50 percent of its annual budget. In 2009, according to an audited financial report, CAI spent just under $4 million building and operating schools in Pakistan and Afghanistan, a sum that includes construction costs, school supplies, teachers' salaries, student scholarships, and travel expenses for program managers. In the same year, CAI spent more than $4.6 million on "Domestic outreach and education, lectures and guest appearances across the United States"—an amount that included $1.7 million to promote Mortenson's books. CAI reported all of this $4.6 million on its tax return as expenses for "programs."

In a confidential memo dated January 3, 2011, an attorney who examined CAI's most recent federal tax return advised Mortenson and the board of directors that CAI's outlays for book advertising and travel expenses for Mortenson's speaking engagements appeared to be in violation of Section 4859 of the Internal Revenue Service Code, which prohibits board members and executive officers of a public charity from receiving an excessive economic benefit from the charity. (From 1998 through April 18, 2011, Mortenson has served as both CAI's executive director and as a board member. From April 2011 until July 2012, the board of directors consisted of Mortenson and just two other individuals.) The memo, written by a lawyer at the firm Copilevitz & Canter, warned:

> Assume that in auditing the Central Asia Institute, the IRS finds that in fiscal year 2009, Mr. Mortenson received an excess benefit from his charity in the amount of $2,421,152.71 (assuming that CAI's advertising expenses related to Mr. Mortenson's books were $1,022,319.71 and travel expenses related to Mr. Mortenson's speaking engagements were $1,398,831 as reported on the organization's 990 for...2009; and further, the charity received none of the revenue that Mr. Mortenson received from said book sales or speaking events).... Further, assuming Mr. Mortenson received the same or similar excess benefit for the previous two years, and the IRS looked back to these years in its audit (as is often the case), Mr. Mortenson could owe CAI up to $7,263,458.13 for excessive benefits received during fiscal years 2007, 2008, and 2009.... [I]f Mr. Mortenson fails to timely pay the correction amount, he could face a total liability ranging from $7,868,746.31...to $23,606,238.62.

An example of the "excessive benefits" provided to Mortenson were several full-page color advertisements in *The New Yorker* to promote Mortenson's books; CAI paid for all of these ads, each of which, according to the magazine's published ad rates, cost more than $100,000. Another example: CAI routinely paid for extravagances such as a four-day excursion by Mortenson to the Telluride Mountain Film Festival in May 2010, where he was a featured speaker. A Learjet was chartered to fly Mortenson, his wife and children, and four other individuals from Montana to Colorado and back. CAI rented multiple residences in Telluride to house the entourage. Lavish meals were billed to the foundation. The jet charter alone cost CAI more than $15,000.

"For a charity that exists to help the poor in the developing world," says Daniel Borochoff, president of the charity watchdog the American Institute of Philanthropy, "this is pretty outrageous behavior. Mortenson is acting as if CAI was his own private business. It's not. He's using the public's money. CAI is a tax-exempt organization subsidized by our tax dollars. It sounds like he's violating every financial practice that nonprofits are supposed to follow. It's very important that any nonprofit separate personal and private business interests from its charitable interests. CAI should not be paying for all these expenses that serve to benefit Mortenson personally. The fact that the charity might also benefit doesn't make it OK."

Mortenson's Pennies for Peace program (P4P) is a commendable cultural studies course that also happens to function as a phenomenally effective marketing-and-fundraising scheme for CAI. By pitching P4P directly to kids, their teachers, and school administrators, Mortenson has induced nearly three thousand schools in the United States and Canada to make P4P part of their standard K–12 curriculum. Hundreds of thousands of children have contributed their lunch money in response to P4P fundraising appeals. "The Pennies for Peace money, every single penny, we put it very quickly to use over in Pakistan and Afghanistan," Mortenson assured these students and their parents during an April 2010 conference presented on Edutopia, the website of the George Lucas Educational Foundation. "All of the money is used for supplies, for books.... Everything is used to help the kids out." In 2009, schoolchildren donated $1.7 million to Pennies for Peace. But CAI's total 2009 outlay for the things P4P is supposed to pay for—teachers' salaries, student scholarships, school supplies, basic operating expenses—amounted to a paltry $612,000. By comparison, in 2009 CAI spent more than $1 million to promote sales of *Three Cups of Tea* and *Stones into Schools*, and another $1.4 million to fly Mortenson around in chartered jets. Donors unknowingly picked up the tab for all of it.

· *Part III* ·
GHOST SCHOOLS

*"But education is a sacred thing,
and the pledge to build a school is a commitment
that cannot be surrendered or broken."*

—GREG MORTENSON,
STONES INTO SCHOOLS

"TAKING GREAT PERSONAL RISKS to seed the region that gave birth to the Taliban with schools, Mortenson goes to war with the root causes of terror every time he offers a student a chance to receive a balanced education, rather than attend an extremist *madrassa*." This trope, from the introduction to *Three Cups of Tea*, is brandished by Mortenson as a central theme in all of his books and in most of his public utterances. The message he seeks to convey is that CAI schools are typically built in areas where fundamentalist madrassas are ubiquitous, and that his schools prevent the nearby madrassas from transforming kids into suicide bombers.

This simply is not true, and Mortenson knows it isn't true. Only a small fraction of his schools are found in locales that might be characterized as breeding grounds for terrorists. In Afghanistan, the majority of schools CAI has established are in areas where the Taliban has little influence or is simply nonexistent, such as the Panjshir Valley and the Wakhan Corridor. In Pakistan, most of the CAI schools are situated in a region the size of West Virginia that used to be known as the Northern Areas but in 2009 was officially designated Gilgit-Baltistan. North of Gilgit-Baltistan lies Afghanistan's Wakhan Corridor; to the northeast, across the towering peaks of the Karakoram, is China; to the southeast is the fiercely disputed border with India—the so-called Line of Control.

Despite its proximity to contested areas of Kashmir administered by India, Gilgit-Baltistan is a tranquil land that has thus far escaped most of the violence afflicting so many other parts of the region. Ethnically diverse, the inhabitants of Gilgit-Baltistan are followers of Shia, Sunni, Ismaili, and Nurbakhshi interpretations of Islam, and "have historically lived in relative harmony," according to Nosheen Ali, a sociologist with a doctorate from Cornell who has conducted extensive research in Gilgit-Baltistan. In a 2010 article titled "Books vs. Bombs? Humanitarian Development and the Narrative of Terror in Northern Pakistan," published in the academic journal *Third World Quarterly*, Dr. Ali writes, "The most troubling irony is that the focal region of Mortenson's work—the Shia region of Baltistan with its Tibetan-Buddhist heritage—has nothing to do with the war on terror, yet is primarily viewed through this lens in [*Three Cups of Tea*]."

"Baltistan is the most peaceful part of Pakistan," Ghulam Parvi confirms. Mortenson hired Parvi in 1996 to be CAI's Pakistan program manager—the organization's first overseas employee. According to *Three Cups of Tea*, Parvi is "known and respected throughout Skardu as a devout Shiite scholar.... 'Without Ghulam Parvi, I never would have accomplished anything in Pakistan,' Mortenson says."

In the summer of 2010, Mortenson, the CAI staff, and the CAI board of directors received a surprising email from Parvi announcing that "he is retired from CAI USA from 30th of June, 2010, due to Greg's unhealthy attitude." Parvi's split with CAI can be attributed to several factors, but at the top of the list is the pervasive dishonesty of *Three Cups of Tea*. "In his book," Parvi explained in a letter to me,

> Greg describes false stories to make the book interesting and sensitive, so that he would become very famous and fund raising make easy. Greg did so and he is really successful in his interior motives. But on the other hand, innocent people working with him in Pakistan, especially in Baltistan, had to face disgrace, loathsome from the society, religiously bashfulness and financial losses. Times and again Greg Mortenson was requested not to perform such acts, which bring bad name and defame to us, but he always very politely and smilingly neglected our requests.

Parvi was extremely disturbed that Mortenson devoted five pages of *Three Cups of Tea* (pages 241–245) to an alarmist disquisition on *Wahhabism* after he purportedly drove past a *Wahhabi* madrassa in the Balti village of Gulapor shortly before 9/11:

> ...Pakistan's most virulent incubator of religious extremism—
> *Wahhabi madrassas....*
> In December 2000, the Saudi publication *Ain-Al-Yaqueen*

reported that one of the four major *Wahhabi* proselytizing organizations, the Al Haramain Foundation, had built "1,100 mosques, schools, and Islamic centers," in Pakistan and other Muslim countries, and employed three thousand paid proselytizers in the previous year....

"In 2001, CAI operations were scattered all the way across northern Pakistan...," Mortenson says. "But our resources were peanuts compared to the *Wahhabi*. Every time I visited to check one of our projects, it seemed ten *Wahhabi madrassas* had popped up nearby overnight."

From someone who presents himself as a steadfast opponent of anti-Muslim bigotry, such fear-mongering is hard to square. According to Nosheen Ali, madrassas are hardly a new phenomenon in Gilgit-Baltistan, nor are they cause for alarm. Such schools have been providing religious education to a variety of Muslim sects for a very long time. But this region, she emphasizes, "is not a terrain teeming with fundamentalist madrassas and Taliban on the loose—the definitive image of the region in [*Three Cups of Tea*]." The subtext of Mortenson's book, she rebukes, is "rooted in a narrative of fear and danger" that's deliberately misleading.

On June 13, 2010, Parvi convened a meeting in Skardu to discuss *Three Cups of Tea*. Some thirty community leaders from throughout Baltistan participated, and most of them were outraged by the excerpts Parvi translated for them. Sheikh Muhammad Raza—chairman of the education committee at a refugee camp in Gultori village, where CAI has built a primary school for girls—angrily proposed charging Mortenson with the crime of fomenting sectarian unrest, and urged the District Administration to ban Mortenson and his books from Baltistan.

Three months after Parvi held this forum, Mortenson received another email warning that he was no longer welcome in Baltistan. It arrived out of the blue from Tanya Rosen, an international lawyer and wildlife researcher with degrees from Bard College, the Università Statale of Milano,

Harvard Law School, and the Yale School of Forestry and Environmental Studies. "Dear Greg," it began,

> I wrote you a couple of years ago back when I was planning
> on going to do some work in the Wakhan. I am primarily
> a scientist working on wildlife and conservation issues but
> obviously in places like the Wakhan such issues go hands in
> hands with development, livelihoods and education. Anyway
> the plan to go to the Wakhan has been postponed for a bit
> because instead friends and colleagues in Gilgit-Baltistan
> asked me to come help with snow leopard conservation work....
> This summer I worked in Hushey, Khandey, Shigar and Baisha
> valleys, Krabathang etc.... The reason I am writing you is that
> the school you built in Hushey is empty and unused (beauti-
> ful by the way) and could not confirm that but people I ran
> into in Skardu and other villages told me that there are other
> schools you have built that apparently are not used. What was
> even more surprising was the fact that many people I talked
> to (about snow leopards) inevitably (because I live in Montana)
> asked me if I knew you and took that opportunity to share a
> series of negative feelings such as: "the book is full of lies", "Dr.
> Greg built the schools but did not provide funding for teach-
> ers, stationery etc.", "he is banned from G-B". Hearing this was
> sad and disappointing, at the same time I know that becom-
> ing successful attracts envy or that sometimes even when you
> are well-meaning things do not turn out the way you want
> them.

Rosen's report that some CAI schools were empty—including the Hushe school, which Mortenson has long trumpeted as one of his most satisfying accomplishments—was disturbing. When I asked Rosen to elaborate, she replied that the elders of Hushe village told her "the school was built by Mortenson and that's where the support ended." It was run thereafter by government teachers, and the "poor quality of education was one of the reasons that the community decided to set up its own private school in a more modest building nearby with a more varied curriculum which includes English."

CAI has become proficient at erecting schools off the beaten path, and Mortenson deserves praise for that. But filling those schools with effective teachers and actually educating children turn out to be much more difficult than constructing schoolrooms. On this front, Mortenson has delivered far less than he has professed.

On April 15, 2010, Mortenson stated during an Edutopia webinar, "The most important thing in any school is obviously a teacher.... So we provide teacher training and support." Students at CAI schools, he assured his audience, "learn to read and write, science, math, everything else. They also, by fifth grade, they learn five languages, including Arabic and English. One of the things we stress is not only that they learn how to read and write Arabic, but they learn how to understand Arabic.... We put a lot of emphasis now on teacher training.... It goes on for a month about twice a year."

Mortenson has made similar assertions on countless occasions, including a Charlie Rose interview broadcast on July 27, 2010. In March 2011, he told a reporter from the Spokane *Spokesman-Review*, "We supply the teacher training and support...we have a teacher-training program and we have emphasized that quite a bit." In the case of the Hushe school, such claims are patently untrue, and they also turn out to be bogus for all but a handful of CAI projects. The statement about students learning five languages is absolutely false, says a CAI staffer, "not even true for a single school." Most teachers, this staffer also reports, have never received any training from CAI.

Even more alarming is the fact that a significant number of CAI schools exist only on paper. Until I pointed it out in April 2011, for example, the CAI website claimed that eight schools had been completed in Afghanistan's Konar Province; during his Charlie Rose interview, Mortenson claimed he'd built eleven schools there. In truth, he'd only built four schools in Konar.

Many CAI schools that actually did get built, moreover, were later abandoned due to lack of CAI support. "Ghost schools," they're called by the disillusioned residents of

Baltistan, where in 2011 at least eighteen CAI buildings stood empty. No one, not even Mortenson, knows exactly how many CAI projects exist as ghost schools, or simply never existed in the first place, because he has repeatedly subverted efforts by his Montana-based staff to track effectively how many schools have been built, how much each school actually costs, and how many schools are up and running. For the CAI staff to gather such crucial information, Mortenson would have to accurately account for how he spends CAI funds—something he has never been willing to do.

Instead, for years the CAI books have been cooked to order. In 2010, for example, when CAI's financial records underwent a long-delayed audit by an independent accounting firm (as the law requires in most of the states where CAI conducts fundraising), the auditor requested documentation from 2009 that showed how much CAI spent on each of its overseas school projects. Such documentation didn't exist, however, so CAI staffers fabricated it. Because they lacked invoices and receipts with which to determine the schools' true costs, in many cases they simply guessed how many students might plausibly be enrolled at each school (or conjured a number out of thin air) and then applied an arbitrary formula based on school size to come up with a fictitious cost for each school. For example, if they imagined a school to have between 300 to 600 students, the school was said to cost $50,000 to build (according to this formula), and its annual operating expenses came to $7,500. Schools reported to have 601 to 1,000 students were said to cost $65,000 to build and $9,000 to operate. By this method, CAI staffers created a fraudulent document and gave it to the auditor. Astoundingly, the auditor accepted the document as genuine, no red flags were raised, and CAI posted the ensuing "Independent Auditor's Report" on its website in May 2010.

★ ★ ★

DURING MORTENSON's Edutopia webinar in April 2010, someone asked him if he still visits Korphe. "I go to Pakistan and Afghanistan three times a year, maybe three to four months a year," Mortenson replied. "I try to go to every school every year." But according to CAI staffers, between 2007 and 2012 Mortenson didn't visit Korphe or anywhere else in Baltistan, and he has never laid eyes on most of the CAI schools. Indeed, many CAI schools have never received a visit from any CAI employee.

To a certain extent, this failure has resulted from insufficient staffing. For the past three years, Mortenson devoted the bulk of his time to getting *Stones into Schools* published, promoting his books, fulfilling remunerative speaking gigs, and fundraising. During this period neither he nor any of his Montana-based employees went to Central Asia to oversee programs firsthand, and his entire staff in Pakistan and Afghanistan consisted of just eleven people responsible for more than a hundred projects, a large number of which require many days of travel, or even weeks, to visit.

The root of the problem, however, lies in Mortenson's dysfunctional management. Whenever CAI staff members have attempted to closely monitor Central Asian programs, some of them report, he's thwarted their efforts. In 2003 and 2004, a woman named Kate DeClerk came on board as CAI's program director. She traveled to Pakistan to document the organization's projects there, and discovered a number of ghost schools. When Mortenson continued to extol these failed projects as proud CAI achievements, DeClerk quit.

After Mortenson refused to comply with CFO Debbie Raynor's repeated requests to provide documentation for overseas programs, Raynor contacted Ghulam Parvi (the Pakistan program manager) directly, instructing him to provide her with documentation. For two or three months Parvi complied—until Mortenson found out what was going on and ordered Parvi to stop. Raynor resigned.

In 2007, Mortenson hired an accomplished consultant to periodically fly to Central Asia to supervise projects. When he discovered irregularities and shared them with Mortenson, Mortenson took no action to rectify the misconduct. In 2010, the consultant quit in frustration.

In September 2007, CAI hired a highly motivated, uncommonly capable woman to manage its international programs. Quickly, she demonstrated initiative and other leadership skills the Institute sorely needed. She had exceptional rapport with Pakistani women and girls. In 2008, she unearthed serious issues in Baltistan that contradicted what Mortenson had been reporting. After she told Mortenson about these problems, she assumed he would want her to address them. Instead, as she prepared to return to Pakistan in 2009, Mortenson ordered her to stay away from Baltistan. Disillusioned, she resigned in June 2010.

When asked about the high turnover of talented employees, a person who worked for CAI during this period replies, "Greg is always fucking with people, intentionally undermining them. That's his management style. He does everything in his power to keep everyone off balance. He did not like people discovering things."

Last June, when Parvi announced his resignation and accused Mortenson of writing "false and baseless stories in the book which is against Islam, Baltistan and Pakistan," Mortenson attempted to discredit Parvi by revealing that in November 2007, Parvi had confessed to embezzling approximately $50,000 from CAI. Mortenson and the CAI board received the confession via email shortly before Parvi embarked on a sacred pilgrimage to Mecca:

I am planning to leave Skardu for Saudi Arabia to perform HAJJ.... A Muslim believes that during Hajj, he has to openly admit all his SINS before the Allah Almighty and seek forgiveness.... Since I have to admit all my bad things, which I had performed without any witness and record, yet I believe Allah Almighty knows. Since there is no excuse, I also want to submit the same situation before you and the CAI Board Members. I admit that willingly or unwillingly I have spent the wealth of CAI at my own. Please Sir, do not hesitate to tell me every thing. I am mentally prepared to make good all losses which I had to CAI.... So Sir, if I am dead and could not come back home, Insha Allah you will not face any problem in getting the available assets of CAI. I have proper record of all the income and expenses of CAI which can be presented before any time.

Upon receiving this email, Mortenson neither fired Parvi nor probed further into his misconduct; according to staffers, doing so would have exposed the existence of ghost schools and other secrets that Mortenson didn't want revealed.

Parvi is not the only CAI employee to have misappropriated funds, and to no small degree Mortenson shares responsibility for the wrongdoing. Over the past two decades, he has disbursed millions of dollars in cash to CAI workers in Pakistan and Afghanistan, and has supervised these employees erratically at best. Brief flurries of intense micromanagement have preceded lengthy periods with no guidance whatsoever. The program director in Kabul went a year without hearing from Mortenson. During one extended silence, Mortenson failed to contact Parvi for an even longer interval. Staff in the Montana office would take calls from Parvi pleading for instructions, begging for Greg to phone him.

Although Mortenson urged his foreign employees to use CAI funds frugally and not waste a single rupee, his deeds contradicted his words. When Mortenson traveled through Pakistan and Afghanistan, he often brought a Pelican equipment case holding bricks of hundred-dollar bills, and he spent huge sums capriciously, frequently on things that seemed to have little or nothing to do with schools. Chartered helicopters flew journalists and VIPs from one end of Pakistan to the other. Favors were asked of powerful individuals, who were rewarded lavishly for their help. When the American office staff implored Mortenson to document his expenses, Mortenson routinely ignored them. Adept at reading their mercurial boss, the overseas staff concluded that cash was abundant and bookkeeping was merely a contrivance done for appearance's sake. As long as Greg went home with inspiring tales to keep the donations flowing, they took for granted that no one would miss a few thousand dollars here and there.

★ ★ ★

IN 2008, Mortenson hired veteran sportswriter Mike Bryan to write a sequel to *Three Cups of Tea*, which was still perched atop the major bestseller lists. By the end of that year Mortenson signed an agreement with Viking Penguin to publish the new book, which didn't yet have a title. The deal included a $700,000 advance to be paid to MC Consulting, Inc., a company Mortenson created in 1998 to shelter his personal wealth.

When Mortenson read a partial draft of Bryan's manuscript in the spring of 2009, he thought it lacked sizzle. So he hired Kevin Fedarko—the journalist who'd authored the *Parade* article that catapulted Mortenson out of obscurity—to rework Bryan's draft and ghostwrite the remainder of the book on an extremely tight schedule. Writing sixteen hours a day for more than a hundred consecutive days, Fedarko completed the job in time for *Stones into Schools* to appear in bookstores twenty-five days before Christmas 2009.[4]

"Picking up where *Three Cups of Tea* left off in 2003," the book's dust jacket announced, "*Stones into Schools* traces the CAI's efforts to work…in the secluded northeast corner of Afghanistan." The story hinges on the challenges Mortenson and his staff must overcome to construct a school in the most remote part of the Wakhan Corridor, a roadless region "where the frigid waters of a shallow, glassy blue lake lap at the edges of a grass-covered field known as Bozai Gumbaz." Here, 13,000 feet above sea level in the Pamir mountains, Kyrgyz herders "struggle to uphold an ancestral lifestyle that represents one of the last great nomadic horse cultures on earth."

Mortenson, who has deft storytelling instincts, had foreshadowed the narrative arc of *Stones into Schools* on pages 250–252 of *Three Cups of Tea*. This passage recounts how, in the fall of 2000, Mortenson happened to be visiting a village in northeastern Pakistan called Zuudkhan, just below a 16,300-foot pass that marked the border with Afghanistan, when a band of Kyrgyz horsemen galloped down from the heights.

> [They] rode straight for him like a pack of rampaging bandits. There were a dozen of them coming fast, with bandoliers bulg-

ing across their chests, matted beards, and homemade riding boots that rose above their knees. "They jumped off their horses and came right at me," Mortenson says. "They were the wildest-looking men I'd ever seen. My detention in Waziristan flashed in my mind and I thought, 'Uh-oh! Here we go again.'"

The leader of the posse, named Roshan Khan, stood nose to nose with Mortenson and demanded, "We know about Dr. Greg build school in Pakistan so you can come build for us?" Khan invited Mortenson to ride back over the pass with him and remain in the Wakhan for the winter as his guest, "so we can have good discuss and make school."

Mortenson explained to Khan that his wife expected him back in Montana in a few days, so he couldn't hie off to the Pamir for the winter. But he silently "swore to himself he'd find some way" to help Khan and his fellow Kyrgyz, and then promised he'd come visit Khan as soon as possible to talk about the school. Satisfied, Roshan Khan jumped on his horse and rode back over the mountains to the Wakhan, where he related the pledge he'd extracted from Mortenson to his father—a venerated figure named Abdul Rashid Khan, supreme leader of the Afghan Kyrgyz, who plays a starring role in the finale of *Stones into Schools*.

In *Stones into Schools* (pages 29–30), Mortenson says his encounter with Roshan Khan occurred in 1999, rather than 2000, and includes a number of details that are at odds with the account in *Three Cups of Tea*. But no matter: According to Mortenson, he had sworn a solemn oath. "Just as *Three Cups of Tea* began with a promise—to build a school in Korphe, Pakistan—so too does Mortenson's new book," proclaims the dust jacket for *Stones into Schools*: "to construct a school in an isolated pocket of the Pamir Mountains known as Bozai Gumbaz."

Sixty-four pages into the book, Mortenson expounds further on his promise to the Kyrgyz:

> Roshan Khan and I enacted a ritual that I recognized from six years earlier, when Haji Ali had stood in the barley fields of

Korphe and asked me to provide an assurance that I was coming back to him. The leader of the Kirghiz horsemen placed his hand on my left shoulder, and I did the same with him.

"So, you will promise to come to Wakhan to build a school for our children?" he asked, looking me in the eye.

In a place like Zuudkhan, an affirmative response to a question like that can confer an obligation that is akin to a blood oath—and for someone like me, this can be a real problem.... Over the years I have missed so many plane flights, failed to appear at so many appointments, and broken so many obligations that I long ago stopped keeping track. But education is a sacred thing, and the pledge to build a school is a commitment that cannot be surrendered or broken, regardless of how long it may take, how many obstacles must be surmounted, or how much money it will cost. It is by such promises that the balance sheet of one's life is measured.

By such promises, indeed. Mortenson's sacred pledge to Haji Ali to build a school in Korphe—to repay the villagers for their charity, and to honor his beloved sister—turned out to be a whopper, calculated to sell books and jack up donations. So too did Mortenson's promise to construct a school in Bozai.

★   ★   ★

FOR THE FIRST PHASE of the Bozai Gumbaz project, Mortenson asked an anthropologist named Ted Callahan to help him. An expert mountaineer and climbing guide, Callahan had recently begun research for a doctoral thesis about the Afghan Kyrgyz, and Mortenson wondered if Callahan would be willing to travel to the Kyrgyz homeland—at the easternmost end of the Wakhan Corridor, part of the so-called Pamir Knot, one of the world's most impressive concentrations of mountains—to work as a consultant for CAI in the spring of 2006. Mortenson explained to Callahan, "I view this as an opportunity where you can help me out, we can help the Kyrgyz out, and I can help you get started with your research." Callahan thought it sounded like a worthy endeavor. He immediately signed on.

CAI had by then built several schools in Afghanistan's Badakshan Province, which encompasses the Wakhan Corridor, but none of the projects was in the high Pamir, where Bozai Gumbaz is situated. Mortenson had never been to the Pamir. There are no roads there. The Wakhan Kyrgyz are nomads who migrate from place to place as they graze their herds. There was no village at Bozai; it was just an expanse of alpine meadow distinguished by a Kyrgyz burial ground and a few mud huts that remained unoccupied most of the year. "My job," says Callahan, "was to get with the Kyrgyz and figure out how to build a school for a nomadic people."

Callahan's initial trip to the Wakhan was not propitious. In Kabul, he met Sarfraz Khan, CAI's program director for northern Afghanistan, who would travel with him through the Wakhan. Right away, Callahan says, "it became obvious that CAI had no official presence in Afghanistan. It was this seat-of-the-pants operation.... Greg had spoken so highly of Sarfraz, but he can't even get us seats on the flight to get up there. He's like, 'We're kind of somewhat unregistered.'" Fortunately, Callahan had attended prep school with the Afghan minister of transportation. He phoned the minister, who arranged for him to book two seats on a flight to Faizabad, the capital of Badakhshan, Afghanistan's northernmost province.

Before they flew north, however, Sarfraz learned that a crew of Pakistani workers he had hired to build some schools had gotten arrested and detained for entering Afghanistan illegally. When Sarfraz's increasingly desperate attempts to get the workers released failed, he begged Callahan for help. Callahan explained the situation to his mentor, Whitney Azoy, an eminent anthropologist who ran the American Institute of Afghanistan Studies, in Kabul. Azoy hosted a dinner for an influential parliamentarian, whom Azoy introduced to Callahan and Sarfraz, and the next day the CAI workers were released. Instead of thanking Callahan for engineering a solution to this serious problem, however, Mortenson became apoplectic. "How dare you compromise my operation!" he blustered.

"It was very odd." Callahan recalls. "Greg was really

pissed off: 'You guys should not have gotten the government involved in this! I do not work with the government! We deal with local power brokers; that's how we get stuff done! You have now invited government scrutiny into our operation! We do not need Whitney Azoy's help with anything!'"

When Callahan told Azoy about Mortenson's reaction to his gracious act, Azoy was struck with an insight: "Maybe Mortenson thinks he's a white knight, riding in to rescue Afghanistan single-handedly," he said. "Afghanistan's full of expats who want to be saviors. Once they get that idea in their heads, there's not room for much else."

By the time Callahan and Sarfraz arrived in Badakhshan and started driving toward the Wakhan Corridor, Callahan's assessment of Sarfraz, at least, had grown more positive. "He's actually a very good guy," says Callahan. As they slowly traveled east down the unpaved, single-lane track, they stopped to inspect several CAI schools under construction, pay laborers for work they had completed, and give them instructions for future tasks. "Things are going pretty well," Callahan says. "Then we get to the end of the road, the last village, called Sarhad-i-Boroghil."

From there they intended to ride horses the final forty or fifty miles to Bozai Gumbaz, but someone had committed a double murder in Sarhad, and the village was swarming with police who'd come to investigate the crime. The police also used the investigation as a pretext to shake down the local citizenry, detaining as a suspect anyone who failed to pay. Because of this tense and potentially dangerous situation, Sarfraz decided to turn around and head back to Faizabad. Not long thereafter, he suffered an acute gallstone attack in the middle of the night, and the ailment appeared to be life threatening.

"He looked like death," Callahan says. "He's puking. He's doubled over in pain. The nearest clinic was probably only ten or fifteen miles away, but 'T.I.A.'—This Is Afghanistan. The jeep that showed up doesn't have working lights and the road is bad." Eventually they arrived at Khundud village, the district capital, where the U.S. Agency for International Development ran a clinic. By then, says Callahan, Sarfraz was "in pretty bad shape. Vomiting a lot. Howling with pain. At the time it seemed pretty dramatic."

Before arriving in Khundud, Callahan had called Mortenson with Sarfraz's satellite phone, and Greg, from his home in Montana, frantically began trying to arrange an emergency helicopter evacuation. The treatment Sarfraz received at the USAID clinic greatly relieved his symptoms, however, and in the morning he no longer seemed in imminent danger. So rather than wait for a chopper, Callahan told Mortenson, "We're going to just keep driving out of the Wakhan." Callahan and Sarfraz headed down the valley with an IV in Sarfraz's arm, and a few days later arrived in the city of Faizabad, where Sarfraz received further treatment and continued to recover.

Still in crisis mode, Mortenson did everything in his power to get Sarfraz on a plane from Faizabad to Kabul, to no avail. So Callahan called Whitney Azoy, who immediately booked seats on a PACTEC flight for both Callahan and Sarfraz, picked them up at the Kabul airport, and gave them a place to stay. After resting, Callahan says, Sarfraz felt fine: "He flashed me his trademark grin and said '*Moshkel nist*'—no problem." Announcing that he would seek a surgical remedy for his ailment when he arrived home, Sarfraz flew to Islamabad the following day. "We said goodbye," says Callahan, "and that was it."

Mortenson provides a much more exciting version of this incident in *Stones into Schools*. In his account (on pages 209–213), when Sarfraz arrived in Faizabad, he learned from a doctor that he had a massive septic infection and needed emergency surgery. A Red Cross plane flew him to Kabul International Airport, where upon landing he was immediately whisked across the tarmac to "a special flight arranged by our good friend Colonel Ilyas Mirza, a retired Pakistan military aviator..., [which] was waiting to fly him to Islamabad. Within minutes of arriving at the Combined Military Hospital in Rawalpindi, Sarfraz was rushed directly into surgery."

"Greg was working the phones hard," Callahan says, "I'll give him that. He didn't sleep for two days. They were calling everyone they knew.... But we got out of there on our own accord."

Callahan left Afghanistan in June 2006. He hoped to return to the Wakhan to complete his report for CAI as soon as possible, but by summer's end he'd heard nothing further from Mortenson about the Bozai project. "Greg is hot and cold," Callahan remarks philosophically. "When you've got his attention you can expect huge email traffic, long phone calls—and then he'll just kind of disappear and go silent."

In September 2006, Callahan was in Bishkek, Kyrgyzstan, where he'd been awarded a fellowship at the American University of Central Asia. There was still no word from Mortenson about going back to the Wakhan, so he returned on his own initiative. After traveling overland from Kyrgyzstan to Tajikistan, he crossed the Amu Darya into Afghanistan and made his way to the high Pamir, where he introduced himself to the storied leader of the Afghan Kyrgyz, Abdul Rashid Khan. For the next two days Callahan remained at the khan's seasonal camp, Karajelga—a clutch of felt-covered yurts near the headwaters of the Little Pamir River, nineteen miles beyond Bozai Gumbaz.

Mortenson devotes most of a chapter in *Stones into Schools* (pages 121–134) to the first and only time he ever met Abdul Rashid Khan—an accidental encounter that occurred in May 2005 in the city of Baharak, fifty miles outside the entrance to the Wakhan Corridor. According to Mortenson, he and Abdul Rashid Khan drew up a formal contract over dinner that stated, in part:

> The Kirghiz people, under the leadership of Abdul Rashid Khan, hereby sign this agreement to build a four-room school at Bozai Gumbaz, Wakhan, with the assistance of the registered charity NGO Central Asia Institute.[9]
>
> Central Asia Institute will provide building materials, skilled labor, school supplies, and help with teachers' salary and training.[5]

Seventeen months after this contract was allegedly signed, when Callahan stayed at Karajelga as Abdul Rashid Khan's guest, he spoke at length with him. When Callahan told the sixty-nine-year-old Kyrgyz leader that an American charity called the Central Asia Institute intended to build a school for the Kyrgyz in the Pamir, Abdul Rashid Khan didn't seem to know who Greg Mortenson was, or have any memory of ever meeting him, says Callahan. "Eventually he pulled out a bunch of business cards, including Greg's, but that might have been the only time Greg ever came up.... I think at some point we all come to look the same to them."

To Abdul Rashid, Mortenson was just another Western do-gooder promising alms. The Kyrgyz leader wasn't inclined to reject such an offer from Mortenson or anyone else—although, says Callahan, he would have preferred that CAI build a road to connect the Kyrgyz to the rest of Afghanistan: "That's what they wanted more than anything else in the world—a road. Second, they wanted some kind of health clinic. Third, as kind of an afterthought, they wanted a school." Their rationale for ranking clinics above schools, Callahan explains, was the appalling infant mortality rate in the Pamir. As one Kyrgyz elder told him, "If 50 percent of the children die before age five, who is there to educate?"

At the time he interviewed Abdul Rashid Khan, Callahan had already visited other Kyrgyz camps to gather information about what kind of school CAI should build, and where. Both Abdul Rashid and his main competitor for influence in the Pamir—an *arbob*, or chieftain, named Haji Osman—were in favor of a boarding school, but nobody wanted to donate a piece of land on which to construct it. "Everybody said that it should be built on someone else's land," says Callahan, "because if it was in one of their own camps, they would have to provide fuel to heat it, and food for the students, and all this other stuff. It sounded like a hassle to them, with little return."

Upon arriving back in Kyrgyzstan to complete his fellowship, Callahan submitted a twenty-one-page report to Mortenson suggesting two sites that seemed appropriate for a CAI school: Bozai Gumbaz and a place called Chelap, nine miles up the valley from Bozai. As for the type of school that should be built, Callahan observed that the nomadic, widely scattered Kyrgyz population argued "in favor of a boarding school, one with a dormitory (plus kitchen) attached to the main body of the school." In the report's conclusion, however, Callahan warned, "CAI will not only face the problem of constructing the schools but running them as well.... It is not at all clear where qualified, motivated teachers could be drawn, but it is certain that they would have to come from outside the Afghan Pamirs." Establishing a successful school that the Kyrgyz would actually use, he continued,

> will almost certainly involve challenges unknown in CAI's prior experience.... If CAI hopes to build more than just the nicest stable in the Pamirs, it will need to continually monitor the schools in order to make sure they are supplied, staffed, and run properly.... For these reasons, CAI should carefully consider its commitment to this project, in terms of time and resources, before any further steps are taken.

★　★　★

WHEN CALLAHAN delivered his report in October 2006, it brought his formal association with CAI to a close. But he returned to Afghanistan in June 2007 to conduct research for his doctoral thesis, and spent fifteen months there. For ten of those months he lived with the Kyrgyz in the Pamir, 13,000 feet above sea level, mostly in the camps of Abdul Rashid Khan.

While traveling to and from the high country, he encountered people in the lower reaches of the Wakhan Corridor whom he had met in 2006, when he'd visited the western end of the Wakhan with Sarfraz. Many of these folks— Wakhi villagers, for the most part—assumed he was still working for Dr. Greg, but "I was quick to disabuse them," Callahan says. They nevertheless deduced that he must know how to contact Mortenson, and they weren't bashful about asking Callahan to forward messages, most of them gripes about CAI schools in the lower Wakhan that remained empty after construction was completed, or schools that had been "built in the wrong place."

The cause of the latter problem, says Callahan, was that villages had "learned to game the system." They understood that if they told Sarfraz or Dr. Greg a woeful story and begged for a school, CAI might build one for them. "The effect was school-building willy-nilly," Callahan explains. The location of existing government schools wasn't taken into consideration. "It was just kind of, build a school here, build a school there. Nobody objected. Everyone was willing to grab any kind of development with both hands."

Acting on the complaints he'd received, in September 2007 Callahan emailed a message to Mortenson:

> At the risk of sounding like I'm meddling in CAI business (in truth, I'm busy enough with my own affairs but this keeps coming up), I thought I'd offer some friendly advice and suggest that you plan a trip to the Wakhan at the earliest opportunity. What goodwill you and CAI enjoy is ebbing fast, with the problems in Sarhad and, now, Kret, and I've been hearing a lot of grumbling and criticism, plus unflattering rumors, about CAI. A visit from you would go a long way towards settling things.
>
> I mention this not because it's any concern of mine but because people know that (in theory) I can contact you and they often ask that I do. Specifically, Ghial Beg, the headman of Kret, is very keen to hear from you, as he's very upset with the status of the school (built but not open, since the MoE [Ministry of Education] won't certify it or whatever).
>
> I'm now living up with Abdul Rashid [Khan] (though on a short break here in Kabul to deal with visa issues). Although I don't want to get involved in the school you're planning to try and build at Mulk Ali in the Little Pamir [the Bozai project], I might be able to provide information if you need any.

Mortenson responded by sending a sarcastic email to Sarfraz suggesting that Callahan was trying to discredit CAI out of spite, or that the complaints he forwarded were based on false rumors planted by the Aga Khan Development Network, a highly regarded foundation that had been establishing successful development projects in the Wakhan long before CAI arrived on the scene, and that Mortenson considered a rival.

★ ★ ★

CONSTRUCTION OF THE BOZAI GUMBAZ school began in the summer of 2008 under the supervision of CAI program director Sarfraz Khan. Ignoring Callahan's recommendation to build a boarding school, Mortenson decided to erect a small, four-room masonry structure, which could be constructed much more easily and much faster. But transporting all the building materials for even a modest building to such a remote location presented enormous logistical challenges. By September 2009, most of these supplies—cement, windows, nails, roofing—had not yet arrived in Bozai, and the only tangible evidence of the school was the stone foundation marking its perimeter. In the final chapter of *Stones into Schools*, to ratchet up the narrative tension, Mortenson speculates that if CAI failed to complete the school before the snows of October brought construction to a halt, the entire Kyrgyz population would become so discouraged that they might "pull up stakes..., gather together their yurts and their animals, and embark on a Final Exodus" from the Pamir.

There is no evidence that the Kyrgyz actually considered such an exodus, however. A more plausible reason for the urgency Mortenson felt to get the school finished by October was that his publisher had promised bookstores that *Stones into Schools* would be on their shelves by December 1, in time for the last few weeks of the holiday shopping season. The Bozai school was the heart and soul of the book. By September 10, when a dozen yaks arrived in Bozai with the first load of building materials, the publisher had already received most of the manuscript. All that remained was the final chapter— which couldn't be written until the school was completed. Anxiety over whether a happy ending would take place in time for *Stones* to arrive at bookstores before Christmas created considerable suspense in the offices of Viking Penguin.

To generate suspense on the page, Mortenson injected the failing health of Abdul Rashid Khan into the narrative. The Kyrgyz leader, who was almost seventy-two years old, was in fact terminally ill. But Mortenson took great liberties when he suggested that Abdul Rashid's final aspiration was to finish the school before his life came to an end:

> As word of his illness spread, men and women all across the Pamir had dropped whatever they were doing and begun walking or riding toward Kara Jilga in order to pay their respects and offer their support. The impulse behind this convergence was touching and appreciated, but it meant that manpower was being drained from Bozai Gumbaz precisely when the need for it was greatest.... "This is no time to sit around watching an old man die," [Abdul Rashid] railed at his well-wishers.... "It is worthless for you to be here when you could be helping to build our future!... This school is our priority.... *Inshallah*, we are going to finish what we have started."

In Mortenson's rendering of Abdul Rashid's last days, nothing mattered to him more than the Bozai school. "Abdul Rashid Khan would have been amused to learn that his dying wish was to see this school completed," notes Callahan, who knew the man well. "He had a wry sense of humor."

Nevertheless, according to Mortenson, when Abdul Rashid implored his people to get the job done before he expired, his exhortations incited them to charge out and win one for the Gipper. More than sixty men, Mortenson wrote,

> rushed to Bozai Gumbaz and flung themselves into the task of assisting the eight [CAI] masons from [Pakistan] who were directing operations. They worked fourteen hours a day hauling water, mixing cement, and roughing out the roof frame.

A week later, the phone rang in Mortenson's Bozeman home. It was Sarfraz calling from Bozai on his satellite phone:

"No problem sir—the school is finished."... It was Monday, September 28. Nearly a decade after the original promise had been made to Abdul Rashid Khan's horsemen, the covenant had finally been fulfilled.

★   ★   ★

A TIDY LITTLE SCHOOLHOUSE now stands in Bozai Gumbaz, and construction was more or less complete by the time Abdul Rashid succumbed to his infirmities in December 2009. But the way things have played out in the real world isn't quite as uplifting as the denouement Mortenson wrote for the book. Bozai, to put it bluntly, may already be a ghost school. Although Mortenson's staff reported on CAI's 2009 tax return (dated May 17, 2010) that sixty-six students were enrolled there, no classes had ever been held in the building. When *New York Times* reporter Edward Wong visited Bozai in the autumn of 2010, he observed,

> the school is still trying to fill its classrooms. Kyrgyz parents prefer that their children herd livestock, said Sarfraz Khan, [CAI's] regional manager. "We need to convince the people to send their children to school," he said.

No students were enrolled at Bozai in 2009 or 2010. Prompted by the negative publicity generated by the *60 Minutes* exposé and the first edition of *Three Cups of Deceit,* CAI reportedly held classes at Bozai for a handful of students during the summer of 2011 and again in 2012; it's unclear whether any classes were held in 2013, or whether classes will be held at Bozai in the future. Furthermore, if the school was built to fulfill some sort of covenant between Mortenson and the Kyrgyz, the Kyrgyz aren't aware of it. Before readers get carried away by the rousing conclusion of *Stones into Schools*, Callahan warned in 2011, they should bear in mind that "Greg met Abdul Rashid Khan once, several years earlier in Baharak. He never spoke to him again. He's never been to Bozai or anywhere else in the Pamir. He has no firsthand knowledge of any of the things he wrote about."

Callahan spent the better part of a year living in the Pamir with Abdul Rashid Khan and his son, Roshan Khan, the horseman with whom Mortenson purports to have made his sacred pledge. "Roshan was one of my best friends up there," says Callahan, "and he never, ever mentioned Greg or the school during the months we spent together, never mentioned a sacred promise. The school was just an afterthought to the Kyrgyz." Callahan doesn't doubt that at some point Mortenson met Roshan Khan in Zuudkhan, just over the mountains from Bozai on the Pakistan side of the border. "But the way Greg tells it," Callahan says, "Abdul Rashid Khan heard that Greg was in Zuudkhan, so he dispatched his son Roshan to plead for a school. That's utter bullshit."

Every September, Callahan explains, the Kyrgyz routinely ride over the mountains to trade at a shrine near Zuudkhan called Baba Gundi Ziarat. During one of these annual trips—most likely in 2000 or 2001—they apparently learned that a wealthy American was in the vicinity, and simply rode over to see what sort of largess they might pry out of him.

Perhaps the saddest aspect of the Bozai saga is that the school Mortenson worked so hard and spent so much to build is never likely to educate a meaningful number of Kyrgyz youth. In his ignorance of the Kyrgyz, Mortenson believed their children would attend the Bozai school in winter, as he indicated in the epilogue to *Stones into Schools*:

> [D]uring the six months when the grasslands lie buried beneath the snow and all connection between the Kirghiz and the outside world has been severed—I am told that there will be roughly 200 children who will study at the school.

In winter, temperatures in Bozai routinely plunge to forty degrees below zero, and the nearest Kyrgyz camp is three miles away. It would take at least an hour to reach the school on horseback through knee-deep snowdrifts. "No one is going to attend that school in the winter," Callahan insists. "Absolutely not." The only time any Kyrgyz actually pitch their yurts in Bozai is from mid-October to mid-December. But the teachers brought to the Pamir by the Afghan Ministry of Education each year arrive in June or July and depart by the end of September. "Education grinds to a halt throughout the Wakhan district in winter," says Callahan. "Even the government-run schools are shut. Everyone is hunkered down. So building a school to provide education in the winter is a bad idea. It's just not going to happen. I'm convinced that the Bozai school was built primarily for the sake of Greg's book, to anchor the narrative."

From June through September, when a teacher could conceivably be hired to teach in Bozai, the summer camp inhabited by Abdul Rashid Khan's clan, Karajelga, is situated nineteen miles away—much too far for any children to attend. Haji Osman's summer camp at Kaschsh Gaz is closer to the school—four and a half miles up the hill, a ninety-minute trudge at an energetic clip—but when Callahan visited Osman in September 2010, Osman told him, "We're never going to use it because it's built down there." The Afghan government provides a teacher who holds classes inside a yurt right in his camp, he pointed out, "so why would our children want to walk all the way down there to go to school, and then have to walk back up at the end of the day? The school is pointless. It's empty. The border police seem to use it sometimes."

Mortenson finally visited Bozai Gumbaz for the first time in October 2012 to pose for photos. Despite having sent word that he would be arriving, the school was closed, no teacher was present, and no classes were being held when he showed up.

★　★　★

IN ALL FAIRNESS, Greg Mortenson has done much that is admirable since he began working in Baltistan nearly twenty years ago. He's been a tireless advocate for girls' education. He's established more than a hundred schools in Afghanistan and Pakistan that have benefited tens of thousands children, a significant percentage of them girls. A huge number of people regard him as a hero, and he inspires tremendous trust. It is now evident, however, that Mortenson recklessly betrayed this trust, damaging his credibility beyond repair.

Still, it might not be too late to salvage the wreckage of Central Asia Institute, which has talented staff and valuable material assets that could further benefit people in the region. But if CAI is to be pulled back from the brink and rehabilitated, the organization must sever its ties with Mortenson. It needs to overhaul its board of directors and find a principled executive director.

While writing this report, as I came to grasp the magnitude of Mortenson's deceit, I felt ashamed at being so easily conned. How could those of us who enabled his fraud—and we are legion—have been so gullible? Ted Callahan attributes the uncritical acceptance of Mortenson and his shtick to the seemingly endless war raging in Central Asia. "The way I've always understood Greg," Callahan reflects, "is that he's a symptom of Afghanistan. Things are so bad that everybody's desperate for even one good-news story. And Greg is it. Everything else might be completely fucked up over there, but here's a guy who's persuaded the world that he's making a difference and doing things right." Mortenson's tale "functioned as a palliative," Callahan suggests. It soothed the national conscience. Greg may have used smoke and mirrors to generate the hope he offered, but the illusion made people feel good about themselves, so nobody was in a hurry to look behind the curtain. Although it doesn't excuse his dishonesty, Mortenson was merely selling what the public was eager to buy.

On April 13, 2011, I sent an email to Mortenson. "Please call me at your earliest convenience," I wrote.

> As I believe you have known for quite a while now, I am writing an article that shines a bright light on you and your management of CAI.... If you'd like to respond to the material

in my article before publication, time is growing very short....
My only conditions for such a conversation are that everything be on the record and that the conversation be digitally
recorded to ensure the accuracy of what is said. I know you are
busy, but the allegations I make in my article are quite serious.
If you wish to tell me your side of the story before my article
is typeset and closes for publication, you need to contact me
without delay.

Eighteen minutes after I clicked the Send button,
Mortenson replied,

I greatly appreciate that you reached out to me now so we can
meet ASAP to answer any questions you have. I'll look at my
schedule today to see when we can make a meeting happen.

Immediately thereafter, Mortenson's personal assistant,
Jeff McMillan, sent an email inviting me to fly to Bozeman to interview Greg on Saturday, April 16. "Thanks, Jon,"
McMillan said, "for the opportunity to let Greg talk openly
and completely before going to press." In subsequent emails, I
confirmed that I had booked my flight and looked forward to
interviewing Greg three days hence.

I heard nothing further from either Mortenson or
McMillan until the afternoon of April 15, when Mortenson
informed me via email, "If we do an interview, I would like
that there is no digital recording. I'm on my way to my doctor
as my oxygen saturation is very low."

I replied,

If we do the interview, it has to be recorded. This point
is non-negotiable. I will, however, promise that
I will not share the audio with anyone else, I will not post
the audio on the Web, and I will not give the audio to
60 Minutes[6] or any other news organization.... I would think
you would want me to record the interview, to ensure the
accuracy of what I write. I will provide a copy of the digital
recording to you.

"We are currently at cardiologist in Bozeman," Mortenson's assistant answered. "Greg is having a heart procedure done Monday morning [April 18] and will not be available for any type of interview." I immediately phoned McMillan to express my concern for Mortenson's health, and to suggest that we conduct the interview by phone instead of in person, at a time convenient for Greg. McMillan said that would not be possible. This was the last communication I received from either McMillan or Mortenson.

I subsequently learned that on April 13, the same day I had emailed Mortenson, *60 Minutes* correspondent Steve Kroft had sent Mortenson and the CAI board of directors a list of questions about whether the charity had received any of Mortenson's book royalties or speaking fees. On April 16, in response to these questions, Mortenson, board chairman Abdul Jabbar, and board treasurer Karen McCown issued a press release in which they made a number of blatantly dishonest assertions, including the following:

> Mr. Mortenson's royalty checks are not split with CAI. Instead, he has donated a percentage of his royalties from the books to CAI. Greg has personally donated hundreds of thousands of dollars to the organization, which includes a percentage of his royalties from his books, and worked for the organization without compensation for a number of years.

The truth, according to CAI's financial records, is that at no point since the charity's inception did Mortenson ever work without receiving a paycheck. And the hundreds of thousands of dollars Mortenson "personally donated" to CAI actually amounted to two checks totaling $420,000 that he had written on April 14, the day after he learned from Kroft's email that *60 Minutes* was about to reveal that Mortenson hadn't given CAI any of the millions of dollars he'd received from his book revenues and speaking fees. When CAI issued the press release touting Mortenson's donations, the checks he'd written to CAI hadn't even cleared the bank.

★ ★ ★

IN MARCH 2011, when I attended Mortenson's lecture in Cheyenne, the experience unsettled me. After taking my seat, while waiting for the program to begin, I read the six-page brochure that had been handed out to everyone in the audience, and I noticed it included the usual lies: the Korphe creation myth, Mortenson's "eight-day armed kidnapping by the Taliban," the claim that for sixteen years he has built schools in "places often considered the front lines of the 'War on Terror.'" The next morning, I called Tom Hornbein to talk about the feelings that seeing Greg in person for the first time in years had stirred. It was Hornbein who initially introduced me to Greg, in 1997, and my description of the Cheyenne event roiled Tom's emotions as well. Reflecting on his own bewildering relationship with Mortenson, he jotted down his thoughts and sent them to me a few hours after our conversation.

"My transcendent emotional feeling is grief for the loss of what might have been," Hornbein wrote. "Like you, I feel as if I was stupidly conned, wanting to believe in the cause and its value and Greg's motivations. Part of me still wants to believe that there was/is something sincere in what he was setting about to do to change the world a bit for the better. Another part of me is just downright angry at his irresponsibility to the cause with which he was entrusted, the lives of so many whom he sucked in and, in effect, spit out, and not least Tara and their kids and other loving bystanders to the play.... I wish I understood the pathology that has compelled the unending need to embellish the truth so flagrantly. With one hand Greg has created something potentially beautiful and caring (regardless of his motives). With the other he has murdered his creation by his duplicity."

· Part IV ·
AFTERWORD: DENIAL

"There has been absolutely no financial misappropriation."

—CAI BOARD CHAIRMAN ABDUL JABBAR,
IN CAI'S *JOURNEY OF HOPE* MAGAZINE, MAY 2011

ON APRIL 19, 2011—twenty-four hours after Byliner published the first edition of *Three Cups of Deceit* as an eBook, and two days after *60 Minutes* aired its exposé of Mortenson's wrongdoing—Montana attorney general Steve Bullock announced that his office was launching an inquiry into Mortenson and CAI, explaining, "We have a responsibility to make sure charitable assets are used for their intended purposes."

Bullock's investigation, completed in April 2012, uncovered numerous "financial transgressions" and revealed that Mortenson's management of CAI was deplorable. The attorney general ordered Mortenson to pay CAI more than $1 million as restitution and forbade him from serving as a voting member of the CAI board of directors or holding any position at the charity "requiring financial oversight." To avoid being sued by the state of Montana, Mortenson and CAI signed a settlement agreement and assurance of voluntary compliance that required CAI to expand its board from three members to at least seven and to hire a new executive director to replace Anne Beyersdorfer, a longtime friend of the Mortenson family who had been serving as executive director since Mortenson took a paid leave of absence shortly after *60 Minutes* aired.

A Washington, D.C.–based public-relations specialist with no firsthand experience in Central Asia or in the field of international development, Beyersdorfer had formerly worked on the political campaigns of Republican presidential and Senate candidates and had served as a media consultant to California governor Arnold Schwarzenegger. From her first day on the job, Beyersdorfer's tenure at CAI was characterized by frequent public statements pledging her commitment to "full transparency" while simultaneously doing everything in her power to keep Mortenson's wrongdoing hidden from journalists, donors, and the public.

It has now been more than three years since the Mortenson scandal erupted. The old board of directors (which consisted of Mortenson and two devoted acolytes, Abdul Jabbar and Karen McCown) was replaced in 2012. A new executive director with solid credentials, David Starnes, took over from

Beyersdorfer in March 2013. But Starnes found it impossible to work with the new board of directors and abruptly resigned on May 13, 2014, dealing yet another blow to the charity's reputation.

Before they were forced out, Jabbar and McCown selected the new board with close guidance from Mortenson, and loyalty to Greg appears to have been one of the main criteria for selection. As a consequence, Mortenson remains on the CAI board as a nonvoting director, he is still paid $169,000 annually (according to financial information released by the charity in August 2014), and he continues to exert considerable influence over CAI operations. Despite the many poor decisions Mortenson has made and the disgrace he's brought to CAI, he remains the public face of the organization.

Mortenson apologists argue that his failings and misdeeds are in the past and should be forgiven. His intentions have always been good, they assert, and the misconduct identified by *60 Minutes*, *Three Cups of Deceit*, and the Montana attorney general was merely an unintentional side effect of the meteoric growth in CAI's revenues resulting from the publication of *Three Cups of Tea*. Mortenson proponents claim that he's not dishonest, just disorganized.

But the available evidence suggests otherwise. As the attorney general's investigative report pointed out, even when Mortenson's managerial failings were brought to his attention, he refused to correct them:

> Based on the information obtained in this investigation, it is clear that Mortenson was not an effective manager of CAI. He, by his own admission, is not well-versed or comfortable in financial and personnel management issues. He did not communicate well with staff in the charity's office in Bozeman.... It is doubtful that even a skilled manager could maintain the kind of travel and outreach schedule Mortenson maintained and still effectively manage an organization that has grown to the size of CAI. Yet, Mortenson consistently insisted on maintaining substantial control over the charity's affairs. When employees challenged him by attempting to get him

to provide documentation to substantiate expenditures, or otherwise to comply with sound management practices, he resisted and/or ignored them.

According to multiple sources, Mortenson routinely sabotaged the efforts of CAI staff to rectify the dysfunction and corruption they encountered. And this appears to be attributable, at least in part, to the fact that Mortenson had secrets he wanted to protect.

New evidence of wrongdoing turns up almost everywhere one looks, but an edifying place to start is the charity's foreign operations, where accurate financial records were seldom kept, and graft is rampant. Contrary to the assurances of supporters who insist that both Mortenson and CAI have cleaned up their acts, an audit of the charity's overseas activities by a Pakistani accounting firm, as well as information provided by other sources in Pakistan and Afghanistan, indicate that CAI's foreign operations are currently beset by widespread corruption. Thanks to appallingly lax oversight that began while Mortenson was in charge and continued during Beyersdorfer's two-year tenure, millions of dollars appear to have been wasted or pilfered by some of the charity's Afghan and Pakistani staff.

★ ★ ★

IN HIS TWO BESTSELLING MEMOIRS, Mortenson frequently sings the praises of his handpicked team of foreign employees. In *Stones into Schools,* Mortenson says of his staff,

> I often refer to this group as the Dirty Dozen because so many of them are renegades and misfits—men of unrecognized talents who struggled for years to find their place and whose former employers greeted much of their energy and enthusiasm with indifference or condescension. But inside the loose and seemingly disorganized structure of the CAI, they have found a way to harness their untapped resourcefulness and make a difference in their communities.

Problem is, several of the "Dirty Dozen" harnessed their "untapped resourcefulness" to loot a staggering amount of cash from CAI. Siphoning funds was ridiculously easy, because nobody from CAI's American office was monitoring how its funds were spent. As a source who used to work for CAI explained, "Greg was accountable to no one, and the staff overseas were accountable to only Greg, but he never held them accountable to anything. Ever. He never checked their books, never asked for receipts."

As a result of the revelations made by *60 Minutes* and *Three Cups of Deceit*, CAI commissioned an audit of the charity's overseas operations for the fiscal year ending on September 30, 2011, which was conducted by a respected Pakistani accounting firm, HLB Ijaz Tabussum & Co., in the spring and summer of 2012. HLB Ijaz examined only a single year of operations, and from the outset they made it clear that their audit should under no circumstances be considered comprehensive; they would merely be auditing "selected transactions as identified by CAI" and would not be conducting "the complete audit or review. The procedures that we will perform will not constitute an audit or a review made in accordance with International Standards on Auditing." One can therefore assume that some financial wrongdoing escaped notice.

Although I haven't seen the entire HLB Ijaz report, significant portions of it (along with numerous corroborating documents) were sent to me by Pakistanis with close ties to CAI who are frustrated by Mortenson's failure to take action against CAI program managers who appear to be misappropriating CAI funds. One of the swindlers exposed by HLB Ijaz was Mortenson's loyal sidekick, Suleman Minhas. Mortenson met him in the summer of 1996, at the conclusion of the trip to South Waziristan on which Mortenson falsely claimed to have been kidnapped by the Taliban. After traveling by car from South Waziristan to Peshawar, the region's major city, Mortenson flew to Islamabad to arrange a flight home to Montana. Suleman, an illiterate but street-smart taxi driver, happened to pick Mortenson up at the Islamabad airport. According to *Three Cups of Tea*:

On the drive to his hotel, Mortenson related the details of his recent detention in Waziristan, and Suleman, enraged that his countrymen had put his guest through such an inhospitable ordeal, had turned protective as a mother hen.... After their taxi had been stopped by a police roadblock on the way to the airport for Mortenson's flight home, Suleman had talked his way past the police with such easygoing charm that Mortenson offered him a job as CAI's "fixer" in Islamabad before getting on his flight.

Some years ago, Mortenson rewarded Suleman for his loyalty (and talent for dispensing baksheesh) by promoting him from fixer/chauffeur to program manager of CAI's operations in Pakistan's Punjab Province. According to the HLB Ijaz audit report, Suleman used this position of authority to unabashedly enrich himself with CAI funds:

- "One-page agreements are made with the contractors for the construction of schools. There are no details regarding start and completion time of work, type of material to be used, and other terms and conditions.... Bills of quantities are not prepared." Beyond these single-page agreements, Suleman maintained no financial records whatsoever.
- None of the construction contracts provided to HLB Ijaz were dated, and, in the words of an auditor, "we are not sure about the amount [CAI] actually spent." For two schools built under Suleman's supervision, no construction contracts were even submitted. According to the audit report, "We have been unable to verify the payment made for the construction of schools amounting to $386,650," because invoices for these payments apparently did not exist.
- In a contract prepared by Suleman for the construction and maintenance of three schools in Pakistan's Azad Kashmir region, after the document had been signed, Suleman added a zero to the cost of one of the projects before submitting it to CAI: The actual cost of the project, 246,500 rupees, was thereby changed to 2,465,000 rupees.
- According to the HLB Ijaz report, "Contracts for the con-

struction of schools were awarded without following any open competitive bidding process," and most of the projects under Suleman's supervision were awarded to a single contractor, Zaheer Hussain Shah, with whom he had a close personal relationship.

• Of the $452,170 that Suleman received from CAI in the fiscal year ending September 30, 2011, he withdrew $207,059 from the bank during the final month of the year. "[C]onsidering the cash flows of banks statements," the HLB Ijaz auditor wrote, "[legitimate] spending of such a huge withdrawal is doubtful, especially in the absence of proper accounting and other record."

• Because Suleman failed to provide auditors with service contracts for teachers, or verification that salaries had been paid, alleged payments of $94,894 to teachers could not be substantiated.

• As instructed by Mortenson, in July 2010 Suleman used CAI funds to purchase a lavish home in an upscale Islamabad neighborhood for CAI staff to stay in when they traveled to Pakistan. But Suleman registered the title to this property in his own name.

★　★　★

OVER THE EIGHTEEN YEARS Suleman has been employed by CAI, it seems he has misappropriated a great deal of the charity's money. But according to the HLB Ijaz audit, other members of the Dirty Dozen also appear to have had their hands deep in the till, including Mortenson's close friend and confidant, Lieutenant Colonel Ilyas Ahmed Mirza, the retired Pakistani Army aviation officer who appears repeatedly in the pages of *Three Cups of Tea*:

> Ilyas was tall and dashing in the way Hollywood imagines its heroes. His black hair silvered precisely at the temples of his chiseled face. Otherwise he looked much like he had as a young man, when he served as one of his country's finest combat pilots. Ilyas was also a Wazir, from Bannu, the settlement

Mortenson had passed through just before his kidnapping, and the colonel's knowledge of how Mortenson had been treated by his tribe at first made him determined to see that no further harm befell his American friend.

In October 2010, Mortenson hired Ilyas to be CAI's "Pakistan chief operations director," a position for which he was paid an annual salary of $42,000, very generous compensation in Pakistan. To carry out CAI's work, Mortenson had asked Ilyas to create a stand-alone Pakistani entity, christened the Central Asia Institute Trust, which Ilyas registered in Islamabad in November 2010. But Mortenson and the CAI board of directors inexplicably allowed the trust to be structured in a way that made it easy for Ilyas to help himself to donated money.

Ilyas and his wife, Talat, were designated the sole trustees, giving them complete control of the trust and all CAI funds that pass through it. According to the HLB Ijaz auditors, "Separate bank accounts for the funds of CAI-USA [i.e., money sent from CAI's American headquarters] are not being maintained. [Funds from CAI-USA] are directly transferred in the personal account of Chief Operations Director [Ilyas]. Non-maintenance of separate bank accounts implies weakness of controls that may result in embezzlement of funds." Indeed, on November 10, 2010—just two weeks after the trust was created—Ilyas paid himself a $50,000 "hiring bonus."

Below is a partial list of the irregularities reported by HLB Ijaz auditors, the CAI Trust accountant, and other sources:

- Following instructions from Mortenson, in May 2011 Ilyas sold the posh Islamabad home Suleman had purchased the previous year. Ilyas reported that he received 47 million Pakistani rupees (approximately $486,000) for the property, which was transferred into the trust bank account. But Ilyas refused to provide auditors with documents related to the sale, so it is unclear how much he was actually paid for it.

According to the trust accountant, Ilyas may have sold the home for more than 47 million rupees and pocketed the difference.

- On September 30, 2011, Ilyas redeemed a CAI certificate of deposit for $42,000 in cash, which, according to the trust accountant, he used for personal expenses.
- According to the HLB Ijaz report, "Contracts for the construction of colleges and schools were awarded [by Ilyas] without following any open bidding process, thus the opportunities of most economical constructions have not been availed."
- According to the trust accountant, the trust paid Ilyas's brother Idrees a salary of $48,000 per year to travel from Islamabad to Bannu once a month to "supervise" construction of a $614,000 library at the University of Science and Technology, the single most expensive project CAI has ever undertaken. The trust also paid the salaries of several of Ilyas's cousins and business associates to work at the UST library project, even though they appeared to do little actual work.
- The trust paid the salary of a cook at Ilyas's personal residence, and the salaries of four drivers to chauffeur Ilyas, his wife, and his daughter around Pakistan in three vehicles purchased with CAI funds. Two of the vehicles were registered in the name of the CAI Pakistan Trust; one was registered in Ilyas's name.

According to a prominent, frequently cited statement on the CAI website,

Each one of Central Asia Institute's projects is locally initiated and involves community participation. A committee of elders guides each selected project. Before a project starts, the community matches project funds with equal amounts of local resources and labor.

But this statement is contradicted by the way CAI actually conducts its business. According to the HLB Ijaz auditor's report,

Selection of projects is at the sole discretion of Chief Operations Director [Ilyas] which raises the risks associated with lack of segregation of duty. There are no selection criteria... either for the selection of place for construction of schools/ college or for providing support for it. Also the effectiveness of the projects is not measurable before or after the implementation.

The Pakistani finance manager for the CAI Trust, twenty-nine-year-old Farhan Jamal Akhtar, has confirmed that most of the projects under the purview of Ilyas were implemented at his whim without community input, often with the aim of providing financial benefits to Ilyas, his relatives, and/or his friends. Mortenson and the CAI board of directors, moreover, seem to have routinely approved projects initiated by Ilyas without exercising much, if any, due diligence.

No less disturbing is the way Anne Beyersdorfer and the CAI board treated Farhan after he courageously reported to the HLB Ijaz auditors that Ilyas was enriching himself from the trust. Ilyas hired Farhan in February 2011, and two months later, when Ilyas showed Farhan the trust deed for the first time, Farhan immediately suspected that his boss was unscrupulous. By then it was too late for Farhan to get his old job back, however. "So I kept on working," he explained to me, "hoping that one day Greg will meet with me and I will be able to tell him everything."

In the spring of 2012, CAI's Montana-based operations director, Jennifer Sipes, asked HLB Ijaz to meet with Farhan to examine the trust's financial records, because Ilyas was in California visiting his son at the time. When Farhan agreed to show the books to the auditors, Beyersdorfer expressed her gratitude in an email:

Salaam and thank you... Ijaz, Pakistan accountants, are reviewing accounting records for money received from CAI-USA during Fiscal Year October 1, 2010 through September 30, 2011... Pakistan accountants are not performing full audit, they are reviewing records for CAI's USA-side auditors. Please let us know any questions or concerns at any time. Many thanks again for your good work, I know your records are very, very good.

All my best... Anne

But Sipes inadvertently forwarded an email she'd received from Farhan to Ilyas, and when Ilyas realized that Farhan was communicating with Sipes and Beyersdorfer about the audit, Ilyas became furious and threatened to fire Farhan if the finance manager had any further contact with CAI's American staff.

Before Ilyas had traveled to the United States, he'd confiscated Farhan's computer and locked it in his office in the hope of keeping the auditors from seeing the trust's complete financial records and ordered Farhan to show them nothing but a fraudulent summary of the books. In an email sent from California, Ilyas made it very clear to Farhan that he should lie to both the auditors and CAI's American staff, saying, "You don't need to be honest with CAI-Bozeman. You only need to be honest with me." Then Ilyas arranged for his brother Idrees to sit in on the audit to ensure that Farhan did not disclose incriminating information to the auditors.

Farhan disclosed everything, regardless, providing the auditors with backup files he'd made of the records on the computer Ilyas had confiscated, because Farhan believed it was his duty. Had he not done so, it's unlikely that Ilyas's wrongdoing would have been discovered.

Farhan—who supports a wife, a two-year-old son, and a father whose health is failing—was nevertheless terrified of losing his job when Ilyas discovered what he'd done. So on June 15, 2012, he sent a confidential email to Beyersdorfer begging her to protect him:

now madam tell me what i can do? how can i secure my job... how can i secure my family future... Madam i am waiting for your reply but again madam please keep secret my mail and

don't share or forward to anyone it is like firing me from job i
hope you can understand.

On October 4, 2012, upon realizing that Farhan had spilled
the beans, Ilyas walked into Farhan's office in a rage, fired him,
and sent an email to Mortenson and Beyersdorfer claiming that
Farhan had quit. Two months later Ilyas filed a lawsuit against
Farhan in Islamabad, charging him with defamation and seeking ten million rupees (about $104,000) in damages. When Bey-
ersdorfer learned of the lawsuit, she sent Ilyas an email, letting
him know that she and the CAI board supported him, and had
arranged for an excellent lawyer to represent him in Islamabad.
She closed her note, "Again, many thanks for your work."

According to CAI financial records, CAI donors provided cash and paid for tangible assets amounting to more
than $1.3 million that wound up in the CAI Trust controlled
by Ilyas. After the HLB Ijaz audit revealed that a significant
portion of this $1.3 million couldn't be accounted for, CAI
asked Ilyas in the summer of 2013 to sign documents that
would transfer control of the CAI Trust to CAI.

Ilyas not only refused to sign the documents; in January
2014, he filed a lawsuit against CAI in Los Angeles County,
California, for breach of employment contract and unfair
business practices, claiming $156,000 in damages. Three
weeks after the lawsuit was initiated, new CAI executive
director David Starnes announced that CAI had "suspended
its relationship with Ilyas Mirza." Because Mortenson and
the CAI board had allowed Ilyas to set up the CAI Trust in a
way that gave Ilyas complete control over it, though, CAI had
no way to wrest it out of his hands. Starnes could do nothing
more than sever CAI's relationship with both Ilyas and the
trust, and stop sending him funds.

In his lawsuit against CAI, Ilyas asserted that he had
done nothing that violates the terms of the trust deed or
the powers assigned to him in a 2011 letter from Mortenson
attesting that "Ilyas Mirza has been appointed by the...CAI
Board of Directors as the CAI CEO in Pakistan." If the letter and related emails from Mortenson to Ilyas are genuine,

Ilyas makes a persuasive case that Mortenson shares culpability for at least some of the CAI funds that were squandered or used by Ilyas for personal gain. In an email dated June 3, 2010, for example, Mortenson wrote,

> Central Asia Institute Board directors have asked me to extend you offer [sic] to be Central Asia Institute Pakistan CEO or director.... We would be very honored if you could help us to set up a HQ office in Islamabad or Rawalpindi responsible for all operations and accountability in Pakistan.... We would like to make sure your salary is better than present.... Suleman and you can find a good house or bangala in Islamabad or Pindi, and then hire good people to get the HQ in order (accountant, steno, chai and chappati cook, chai server, reception (Inshallah a woman) etc.

In an email dated June 22, 2010, Mortenson told Ilyas,

> I'm not sure what we should start your pay at? $3,500 per month or more? Let me know, as I don't have any clue. I also want our Board to agree to give you a $50,000 hiring bonus.... Let me know what you think, you are important for CAI future.

And on October 19, 2010, Mortenson wrote,

> CAI should purchase you two vehicles.... I would advise getting one for city driving in Islamabad, and then another one... for trips to Azad Kashmir etc. Please put the city vehicle in your name and the [other] in CAI name.... Please also set up one bank account in Pakistan in your name (and Central Asia Institute if they allow), so we can start to wire funds to you.... You are a big inspiration for me since the first time we met. You are dear friend and brother, and always in my prayers and thoughts. Thanks for taking on the duties.

Ilyas's lawsuit against CAI was dismissed in June 2014, but the CAI Trust and all its remaining assets continue to exist under Ilyas's control. And Farhan's reward for blowing the whistle on Ilyas? Farhan was thrown under the bus, as if he, rather than Ilyas, had been the one ripping off CAI. Broke and unemployed, Farhan was abandoned by Mortenson, Beyersdorfer, and the CAI board and has had to rely on his own resources to face the lawsuit Ilyas filed against him in Pakistan. Although the defamation claim against Farhan appears to be baseless, Farhan was forced to sell his father's property to pay an attorney to defend him against the lawsuit, which, as of September 2014, was still wending its way through the Pakistani courts. According to Farhan, his father received an explicit warning that Farhan should be careful or he might be murdered. The individual who made the threat told Farhan's father, "We know where he work, from where he use public transport and on which ways he go home."

"App ka dua go," Farhan implored me in an email written in his native Urdu: "Pray for me."

★ ★ ★

THE PROBLEM OF CAI employees pilfering donated CAI funds isn't limited to the charity's overseas staff. Upon examining CAI's credit card statements for eight sample months from 2001 through 2010, the Montana attorney general determined that

> CAI provided receipts for just 38 percent of the total charges....
> [For many of the receipts] there was no voucher or other written indication of the purpose of the charge. Mortenson, in particular, consistently failed to comply with either commonly accepted business practices or CAI's policy manual with respect to documenting expenses charged on CAI's accounts.... Board members testified that despite requests, cajoling, demands and admonitions, they were unsuccessful in getting Mortenson to submit proper documentation to support the charges he was making to the charity....
>
> The more significant issue was...the nature and magnitude of charges for which inadequate documentation exists. Through the years, Mortenson charged substantial personal

expenses to CAI. These include expenses for such things as L.L. Bean clothing, iTunes, luggage, luxurious accommodations, and even vacations.

The attorney general found that Mortenson charged $75,267 in personal expenses to CAI in 2010 alone. All told, from 2004 through 2011, Mortenson used CAI credit cards to pay for more than $214,000 in personal expenses. His defenders have tried to explain away his personal use of donated funds as an innocent oversight, a by-product of the turmoil generated by CAI's spectacular growth. But that dog won't hunt. The surge in CAI revenues wasn't an unforeseen accident that took Mortenson and his board by surprise. As Mortenson clearly states in *Stones into Schools*, it was part of a deliberate plan. Following the publication of *Three Cups of Tea*, Mortenson went to extraordinary lengths and spent a colossal amount of donated money to promote himself and his book. According to the attorney general's report, from 2006 through 2011, CAI, a nonprofit charity, spent approximately $5 million to advertise *Three Cups of Tea* and *Stones into Schools* and another $4 million to buy copies of the books to give away, even though the charity didn't receive a nickel of the royalties from Mortenson's books.

During the years in question, CAI also spent approximately $2 million flying Mortenson on private jets to over 150 paid speaking engagements. When members of the public noticed Mortenson traveling on chartered jets, he would tell them the aircraft had been provided free of charge by the CEO of Costco or some other benefactor.

CAI points to the $70 million in donations it received from 2006 through 2011 to justify the $11 million the charity spent promoting Mortenson and his books. But this argument fails to consider that Mortenson's publisher, the Penguin Group, received a similarly large, if not larger, windfall from book sales generated by the CAI advertising campaign. Penguin let CAI pay for those expensive ads, even though the cost of promoting a book or an author is properly borne by the book's publisher or the author himself, not a charity's tax-subsidized revenues. It's unconscionable that Mortenson and his board of directors allowed Penguin to enhance its bottom line with funds donated to educate destitute Afghan schoolchildren. And to add insult to injury, the books Penguin foisted on the public with CAI's advertising dollars were larded with lies.

One should also bear in mind that it wasn't only CAI and Penguin who hit the jackpot thanks to, among other things, what turned out to be a deceitful marketing campaign funded by unsuspecting CAI donors. Contrary to claims by Mortenson, his publicists, and his supporters, Mortenson got rich, too. One frequently hears his advocates saying such things as, "If Greg is misappropriating funds, then show me the luxury cars, fancy boats, and closets full of shoes." Or, "He still lives in a modest two-bedroom house in a middle-class neighborhood in Bozeman." Yes, Mortenson still lives in that house. But several years ago he purchased the homes on both sides of it, and then spent $900,000 transforming two of the three residences into an elegant family compound.

We don't know exactly how much Mortenson's personal wealth increased as a result of the expensive marketing campaign underwritten by CAI, because Mortenson's lawyers waged an expensive and ultimately successful battle to prevent the attorney general from divulging anything about Mortenson's personal finances. In a grimly ironic twist, CAI donors thus paid Mortenson's lawyers to keep them from discovering how much Mortenson has enriched himself at their expense. And make no mistake: CAI donors have paid Mortenson's lawyers astronomical sums over the past few years and may be on the hook for similarly immense legal bills in the years ahead.

In the fiscal year ending September 30, 2010 (i.e., before the *60 Minutes* exposé), CAI spent just $28,170 on attorneys' fees. Between December 1, 2010, and December 1, 2011, by comparison, it spent more than $1.7 million on attorneys' fees and other costs associated with two legal disputes: the Montana attorney general's investigation; and a class-action lawsuit over the fabrications in Mortenson's books that was dismissed before the court examined the evidence, due to procedural flaws in his adversaries' complaint. In 2012 and 2013, CAI spent an additional $2.1 million on attorneys' fees. CAI's legal expenses are so high because the CAI board of directors retained four law firms to represent Mortenson and the charity, including a San Francisco firm that billed CAI at rates as high as $1,105 per hour and a Washington, D.C., firm that billed as much as $645 per hour.

★ ★ ★

WHEN ARGUING THAT Mortenson's wrongdoing should be forgiven, his supporters have pointed out that thousands of children in Pakistan and Afghanistan wouldn't have received an education were it not for his efforts. This is a compelling argument. Indeed, had Mortenson owned up to his mistakes after the scandal came to light, I would have been among the first to forgive him. It's hard, however, to pardon someone who refuses to acknowledge the harm he has caused. It's impossible to trust someone who tries to explain away his lies by telling more lies. Mortenson's ham-fisted, disreputable management of CAI hasn't merely wasted millions of dollars in donations subsidized by taxpayers. It's also done incalculable damage to important CAI programs and the people they were supposed to help. And Mortenson's dishonesty hasn't harmed just CAI; it has diminished trust in other nonprofit aid organizations around the world.

On January 14, 2014, Tom Brokaw, the respected television anchorman and éminence grise at NBC News, interviewed Mortenson on the *Today* show—the first media interview Mortenson had granted since the immediate aftermath of the *60 Minutes* broadcast in April 2011. Brokaw pointed out to Mortenson, "You have said that you made mistakes. There were lots of questions about accounting that go well beyond just mistakes."

Mortenson tried to sidestep Brokaw's imputation, suggesting that there was nothing sinister about his diverting more than a million dollars of donated funds to his personal bank account—that it was just an inadvertent lapse: "I always have operated from my heart. I'm not a really head person [*sic*]. And I really didn't factor in the very important things of accountability, transparency."

Later in the interview, Mortenson said, "I've talked to people who were very adamant that I make changes; I've apologized to them. I'd also like to apologize to everybody. I let a lot of people down.... In a maybe strange, ironic way, I'd like to thank CBS and Jon Krakauer, because had they not brought these issues up, we could've gotten into more serious problems."

But Mortenson's televised display of contrition went no further than these fuzzy, indistinct expressions of regret. He didn't accept responsibility for any specific acts of wrongdoing. The insincere expression of gratitude to CBS and me on the *Today* show notwithstanding, Mortenson continues to portray himself as the victim of a witch hunt, and he and his defenders continue to state, loudly and often, that by revealing his managerial failings and raising questions about his integrity, *60 Minutes* and I have done irreparable harm to schoolchildren in Central Asia. As evidence of this harm, Mortenson and his defenders point to the dramatic reduction in donations to CAI in the aftermath of our exposés. It seems not to have occurred to them that the falloff in donations might be a sensible reaction to the widespread malfeasance that has been exposed—wrongdoing for which Mortenson is clearly to blame.

As Daniel Borochoff, president of the charity watchdog American Institute of Philanthropy, noted in August 2011,

> There is no doubt Greg Mortenson should be given credit for doing arguably more than anyone else to bring attention to the dearth of education for children, especially girls, in central Asia. He also deserves credit for the functioning schools built and funded by his charity. But these good deeds do not let him off the hook for using CAI to absorb millions in expenses that generated personal profits for himself and his books' publisher.... These actions, combined with the alleged

inaccuracies in *Three Cups of Tea*, have breached donors' trust to a degree that CAI will be unable to recover from, in AIP's opinion, with Mortenson at the helm.... For a man who has dedicated so much of his life to promoting CAI's important cause, Mortenson's resignation letter to the charity is perhaps the most generous contribution he could now make to the people of central Asia.

★　★　★

KEVIN STARR IS A PHYSICIAN who serves as managing director of the Mulago Foundation, a charity "focused on health, poverty, and conservation in the world's poorest places." While working in Afghanistan's Wakhan Corridor in 2008, Starr encountered some empty schools built by CAI and asked people who lived nearby why the buildings were empty. Their replies inspired him to write the following in a 2011 blog posted by the *Stanford Social Innovations Review*:

[L]ocal villagers portrayed Greg and CAI as cowboys who parachuted in and didn't listen. Now they had schools in the wrong places and no one to teach the kids.... People seem most outraged by the apparent fabrications in [*Three Cups of Tea*]... but the real crime is that CAI appears to have raised 60 million dollars and doesn't have that much to show for it. No one really knows how many schools are actually up and running. CAI says 170; my own tiny random sample and the *60 Minutes* investigation indicate that there are probably a lot less. Even if you allow for a generous figure of 150, that represents $400,000 of donor money per school. That's ridiculous.... The Agha Khan Development Network built 280 schools in a small corner of the same region and achieved more than 95% female literacy—for a fraction of the cost. The argument about what's fabricated and what's not will rage on for a while, but what we really should be asking is how did CAI spend so much to accomplish so little and why did people keep giving Greg money?... [*New York Times* columnist] Nicholas Kristof and others offer the classic noble-visionary-as-poor-manager defense, portraying Mortenson as a flawed hero who nonetheless accomplished great things. He didn't.... "Creating awareness" is not the same as creating impact, and it too easily becomes a black hole that seems to justify almost any expenditure.

Starr suggests that Mortenson's false representations of what CAI has accomplished are a more serious cause for concern than the lies in his books about being kidnapped by the Taliban or climbing Himalayan peaks that he never set foot on. He's right, but all these falsehoods are of a piece. Each reflects Mortenson's inveterate dishonesty.

Concerning his books, Mortenson has continued to insist they are truthful accounts, despite overwhelming evidence to the contrary. In an interview Mortenson gave to *Outside* magazine in April 2011, editorial director Alex Heard asked, "Greg, the *60 Minutes* segment claimed that there are major fabrications in *Three Cups of Tea*. Are there factual errors in the book, and if so, how did they get there?" During his meandering, evasive reply, Mortenson suggested that any errors were nothing more than literary license:

> It's really complicated, but I'm not a journalist. I don't take a lot of notes. David [Oliver Relin] and I collaborated. He did nearly all the writing, and along with hundreds of interviews of those involved in the story, I helped him piece together the whole timeline, and from that we started creating the narrative arc and everything....
>
> What happens then is, when you re-create the scenes, you have my recollections, the different memories of those involved, you have his writing, and sometimes things come out different. In order to be convenient, there were some omissions. If we included everything I did from 1993 to 2003 it would take three books to write it. So there were some omissions and compressions.

Unconvinced, Heard tried to pin Mortenson down about the veracity of the CAI creation myth described in the first eight chapters of *Three Cups of Tea*, which relies on Mortenson's claim that he stumbled into Korphe in 1993 after taking a wrong fork in the trail. "But you stand by the Korphe story as it was written?" Heard probed.

"Well, there are discrepancies that, again, have to do with compression of events," Mortenson replied, while remaining adamant that these "discrepancies" didn't impugn the essential truth of his story. Mortenson explained that he spent the final night of his trek down from K2 with Scott Darsney and their two porters, Yakub and Mouzafer, at the site of an old Pakistani Army camp near the snout of the Biafo Glacier, which is seven miles above Askole. "The next morning," Mortenson said,

> "I was so weak that I pretty much ditched everything I had. We started walking at around 10 or 11, I got left behind as usual, and I was alone when I hit a fork in the road. When you're coming out from there, there's a fork in the trail about two hours before Askole, a village where expeditions park their jeeps when they hit the trailhead. If you go... to the left—which I did—it goes to Korphe. The main trail goes right... heading to Askole. I made a wrong turn there. So I ended up in Korphe. I was met there by Haji Ali, the village chief.
>
> I got to Korphe, I would say, early afternoon.... I remember collapsing by the inner hearth of his house. I thought I was in Askole, but they said, No, you're in Korphe.
>
> I was there a few hours, probably two or three hours, had tea, and I said, I gotta go to Askole. They took me to a cable-pulley bridge over the Braldu River."

There is an insurmountable problem with this account. The well-established trekking route from the Baltoro Glacier down to Askole follows the north side of the Braldu River the entire way, without ever crossing it. Korphe is on the other side of the river—the south side. In 1993, according to Masood Ahmad, a Pakistani American educator and mountain guide who trekked from the Baltoro Glacier to Askole approximately two weeks after Mortenson, "I can also categorically and unequivocally state that there was NO bridge across the Braldu River between Askole and Korphe in 1993, as I was there during the same time Greg Mortenson was." Regardless of whether Mortenson took a wrong fork in the trail, there is absolutely no way he could have ended up in Korphe unless he swam across the Braldu—which is roiled by rapids and paralyzingly cold.[7] On pages 22–23 of *Three Cups of Tea*, this is how Mortenson describes the river as he stepped off the terminus of the Baltoro Glacier and saw the Braldu's headwaters rushing from beneath the ice:

> The snout of the Baltoro Glacier lay at the bottom of a canyon, black with debris and sculpted to a point like the nose of a 747. From this aperture, the subterranean rivers traveling under sixty-two kilometers of ice shot into the open with an airblast like a jet engine's exhaust. This foaming, turbulent waterspout was the birthplace of the Braldu River. Five years later, a Swedish kayaker arrived with a documentary film crew and put in at this same spot, attempting to run the Braldu to the Indus River, all eighteen hundred miles to the Arabian Sea. He was dead, smashed against boulders by the primordial strength of the Braldu, minutes after he hit the water.

Given his debilitated condition after his ordeal on K2, it strains belief to suggest that Mortenson would have even considered swimming across the Braldu. Had he attempted it, he almost certainly would have drowned, and if by some miracle he had survived, it's inconceivable that he would have neglected to describe the feat in *Three Cups of Tea*. Belatedly recognizing the patent impossibility of his claim to have reached Korphe by the route he described above, several months after *Outside* posted his interview with Heard, Mortenson had CAI's communications director, Karin Ronnow, present an entirely different story about how he ended up in Korphe[8] in an article published in CAI's annual magazine, *Journey of Hope*. In this new account, Mortenson didn't make a wrong turn "two hours before Askole"; instead he continued down the obvious trail to Askole and then, immediately before entering that village, inexplicably abandoned it, took a sharp turn to the left, and walked across a little-known suspension bridge, which he then neglected to mention over the years that followed.

During a visit to Korphe in May 2011, Ronnow wrote, she and several companions were taken to see this bridge by Twaha, the son of the late Haji Ali. As readers of *Three Cups of Tea* will recall, both Twaha and Haji Ali figure prominently in Mortenson's narrative, have benefited greatly from his largesse, and regard him as family. In Ronnow's telling, it was late afternoon when Twaha guided her

> through the narrow maze of paths between the houses. He pointed out his own home and then his father's home, where he said, "Inside there is where Greg slept. We could make museum someday. What do you think?" . . .
>
> The path wound north alongside irrigated fields, across a rock-strewn stream and onto an arid plateau littered with boulders.
>
> From the village, it's a thirty-minute walk to the remains of the old bridge over the Braldu River Twaha was so eager to point out.
>
> "There," he said, pointing down a nearly vertical hill. "The bridge is right there. Bridge is no good now, but when Greg came [in 1993], it was crossable. If you were over on the other side and looked south, you would see Korphe, but not Askole. So he crossed to Korphe."
>
> And the rest, as they say, is history.

Contrary to this assertion by Ronnow, however, the rest was not history. It was merely another attempt by Mortenson to deceive.

The derelict bridge mentioned in Ronnow's article does indeed exist. Although it's been all but destroyed by seasonal floods and more than a decade of neglect, if you find Korphe on Google Earth and zoom down to a point 1.1 miles due east of the Korphe school, you can plainly see what's left of the ruined span. The southern terminus of its fraying cables is anchored to the edge of a broad alluvial shelf overlooking the Braldu River. This "arid plateau littered with boulders," as Ronnow describes the setting, is known to the residents of Korphe and Askole as Testay Dass.

Twaha, though, was plainly mistaken (or was egregiously misquoted by Ronnow) when he said that Mortenson reached Korphe by walking across this bridge in 1993. Such a feat would have been impossible, because the bridge didn't exist at the time.

Balti workers who built the bridge at Testay Dass say that construction didn't begin until 1999, and wasn't completed until 2000. And here's the kicker: It was Mortenson who personally arranged for this bridge to be built and paid for with CAI funds, according to Zaman Ali, a resident of Askole who helped build it. Other Pakistani sources have confirmed that in 1999, four years after Mortenson built the bridge made famous in *Three Cups of Tea,* he began building a second bridge east of Korphe at Testay Dass.

After I revealed that Mortenson's claim to have reached Korphe in 1993 by this bridge was as preposterous as his earlier claim to have ended up in Korphe because he took a wrong fork in the trail, he said nothing more about crossing a bridge that didn't exist. Instead, he floated yet another tale to explain how he crossed the Braldu on his trek down from K2.

In 2012, Mortenson traveled to Korphe for the first time in several years. During this visit, according to a Korphe native, Mortenson invited all the residents of Korphe, Testay Dass, and a nearby settlement known as Tinu to a feast. Mortenson had Twaha buy a cow and cook the meat. Then, while the villagers were eating, he offered five hundred rupees—slightly less than five dollars—to anyone who would testify there was a bridge across the Braldu River at Testay Dass in 1993. "The temptation is big," explains a woman whose husband is from Korphe. "This is the thing. Life in Baltistan is so hard."

Fast-forward to the summer of 2013. Mortenson returned to Korphe with a two-person film crew from Utah: Jennifer Jordan, the director, and her husband, videographer Jeff Rhoads. On her website, Jordan describes Mortenson as "her friend and colleague." She and Rhoads had accompanied him to Baltistan to make a documentary titled *3000 Cups of Tea*, which was intended to refute the allegations made by *60 Minutes* and me about Mortenson's lack of probity. Before their departure, Mortenson told Jordan he would introduce her to local men who would testify on camera that there was a bridge across the Braldu River in 1993. When they arrived in Korphe in September 2013, as promised, Jordan and Rhoads were taken to interview two individuals who told them exactly what they had traveled so far to hear.

In February 2014, after her return to Utah, Jordan sent me an email asking if she could interview me on camera for her film. When I asked her several pointed questions to help me decide whether I could trust her to accurately represent my views ("Do you think *Three Cups of Deceit* is accurate in its criticisms of Greg? If not, what are the three most serious inaccuracies?"), she dodged them. Instead she replied, "[I]t is my job as a journalist and filmmaker to investigate the story, no matter where it leads.... I do not have an agenda here."

Three weeks later, on March 13, Jordan posted a tendentious seven-minute trailer on the Internet to raise money for *3000 Cups of Tea*. When the trailer initially went online, it opened with a riveting montage of brief video clips, each only five to ten seconds long, of various talking heads delivering withering criticisms while a mournful dirge plays in the background. Among the individuals featured in this opening montage were Mortenson's wife, Tara Bishop, fighting back tears of anger; an outraged Abdul Jabbar, the former CAI board chairman who was forced to resign by the Montana attorney general; and Marvin Kalb, the distinguished journalist and television news anchor, speaking with concern about the sins of present-day journalists. The montage was skillfully edited to lead viewers to believe that each of these individuals considers the *60 Minutes* Mortenson exposé to be despicable. On March 23, however, a new iteration of the trailer replaced the first version, and in this revised version the clip of Marvin Kalb had been deleted.

It turns out that the clip vanished as a result of an email

Kalb sent to Jordan on March 21. They had been friends since the late 1980s, when Kalb was director of the Shorenstein Center on the Press, Politics and Public Policy at Harvard's Kennedy School of Government and Jordan was director of the Forum—the Kennedy School's prestigious venue for public speakers. The subject line of Kalb's email to Jordan read, "unhappy." The body of the message explained,

> When you first called asking for an interview, I told you I had not seen the *60 Minutes* piece and therefore could not comment on it. You answered that you needed someone to comment on TV news, not the piece. I agreed after you persuaded me that I would not be used as a counterpoint to *60 Minutes.* During the interview, quite long as I recall, you did toward the end ask questions about *60 Minutes,* and I did not answer them—to your distress, as I recall.
>
> Weeks later, you sent me a video copy of a fundraising trailer, which had no mention of me in it, no image of me in it, and now I see another version of that same trailer, which does include me. That is extremely disappointing.
>
> I do not allow myself to be used in fundraisers, not by Harvard, not by the Pulitzer Center, where I am Senior Adviser on, among other things, journalistic ethics, and not even by Brookings, where I am a Senior Fellow. Now I am used in a video fundraising trailer, and in a context that puts me in criticism of a broadcast that I told you I had not seen and therefore could not comment on.
>
> If our old friendship at the Kennedy School means anything to you, I ask you to please immediately drop me from your fundraising trailer and from your upcoming documentary. I want nothing to do with either.

The current iteration of the trailer is exactly the same as the original version, minus the footage of Kalb. The opening montage concludes with a seven-second clip of CAI board member Farid Senzai tearfully declaring, "If the intentions are to just destroy the reputation of an individual, then people like that need to be fought back."

A couple of minutes later, Mortenson appears on-screen to admonish, "What really bothered me was, it seemed like there was more intent to try and destroy me, with no regard for the children overseas."

"The media can make or break you in a matter of minutes," intones Abdul Jabbar, "and all the fact-finding, the truth, they can be just shelved, thrown out."

Jordan—who narrates the film in addition to directing it—looks scornfully into the camera and declares, "One of the most damning allegations [made by *60 Minutes* and Krakauer] was that Greg lied in his book *Three Cups of Tea*, in going to Korphe on his way out of the mountains."

The trailer cuts to a clip from the *60 Minutes* broadcast of me telling Steve Kroft, "It's a beautiful story, and it's a lie."

Jordan then delivers what she intends to be the knock-out punch: "Once on the ground in that tiny village at the end of the road, we learned that every villager we spoke to remembered Greg from twenty years before. We even found the men who were then boys playing on the riverbank, and they saw Greg coming over the bridge, stumbling out of the mountains." As Jordan speaks, a video clip shows the two men she interviewed the previous September, affirming there was a bridge across the river in 1993.

Shortly thereafter, a charming young blogger named Sabina Khan tells Jordan, "I couldn't wrap my head around why *60 Minutes* or Krakauer would make these accusations without doing their research."

"No good deed goes unpunished," explains new CAI board member George McCown, the husband of former board treasurer Karen McCown.

One of the last acts by Karen McCown and Abdul Jabbar before they were forced to resign by the Montana attorney general in July 2012 was to appoint Farid Senzai and six other new members to the board of directors. These new directors subsequently appointed George McCown to the board in 2013, and bestowed the title "emeritus advisor" on Karen McCown and Jabbar. Although Mortenson was stripped of his voting rights by the Montana attorney general, the new directors invited Mortenson to remain on the board as an "ex-officio" member. Thus, contrary to the attorney general's intent when he ordered that the entire board be replaced with a slate of independent directors, the new board is still influenced by the same individuals who, for most of the past decade, sat in the back seat singing Mortenson's praises as he steered CAI over a cliff. If the trailer is any indication, many of the new board members appear to be as blindly loyal to Mortenson as the old board members.

★ ★ ★

AS JENNIFER JORDAN'S TRAILER SUGGESTS, a makeshift bridge does occasionally span the Braldu River at Testay Dass, but only in the dead of winter. The residents of the village own a sixty-foot wooden plank. When the temperature stays below freezing for an extended period—preventing the snowpack in the mountains upstream from melting, thereby causing the river level to drop dramatically—they lay the plank across the Braldu between boulders exposed by the diminished flow. This is never possible, however, except in midwinter, during sustained periods of bitter cold.

So Mortenson could not have crossed the Braldu on this temporary plank bridge in the summer of 1993, as he now claims in this most recent of several contradictory versions of how he arrived in Korphe. He completed his trek down from K2 at the beginning of September, when the weather is warm and the Braldu is still running too high for the crucial boulders to be safely above the waterline. Residents of Korphe who are not beholden to Mortenson have assured me that the plank bridge has never been deployed in September; thus it would have been impossible for Mortenson to use it to reach the village in 1993.

At the time of his April 2011 interview with Alex Heard, published online by *Outside,* Mortenson had not yet concocted a narrative about crossing the Braldu on a suspension bridge of his own construction, or invented his subsequent tale of striding above the river on an imaginary wooden plank. And Heard failed to note the obvious impossibility of Mortenson's earlier claim of having wandered into Korphe after taking a wrong turn. But Heard recognized that the story Mortenson told him was quite different from the account of the same events presented in *Three Cups of Tea*.

"In the book," Heard pointed out, "you're described as being in Korphe overnight, but now you think you were really there only a few hours."

According to *Three Cups of Tea*, in 1993 Mortenson spent many days and nights in Korphe, recovering his health in the home of Haji Ali after failing to climb K2. At the conclusion of this extended visit, as recounted in a pivotal scene in the book, Mortenson placed both his hands on Haji Ali's shoulders and, in the name of his deceased sister, famously made a pledge that brought tears to the eyes of millions of readers: "'I'm going to build you a school... Mortenson said. 'I promise.'"

"When did that actually happen?" Heard demanded.

"The...scene in Korphe about building a school happened in September 1994, a year later," Mortenson acknowledged.

In fact, this statement isn't true, either, because Mortenson didn't return to Pakistan until November 1994, and probably didn't actually visit Korphe for the first time until March 1995. But during his interview with Heard, Mortenson nevertheless confessed that in 1993 he was in Korphe for at most "a few hours," and during that visit he didn't promise Haji Ali or anyone else that he would build a school there. Which confirms that the most consequential anecdote in *Three Cups of Tea*, around which the rest of the book unfolds, is a fabrication. To appreciate the magnitude of this lie, one should re-read the first eight or nine chapters of the book while bearing in mind that Mortenson, by his own admission, didn't spend a single night in Korphe after trekking out from K2.

Yet, incredibly, Mortenson insisted during his January 2014 interview with Tom Brokaw that the events described in his books are true. Mortenson declared on national television, "I stand by the stories. The stories happened." And in a September 2014 interview with Associated Press reporter Matt Volz, recorded on videotape, Mortenson repeated the claim: "I stand by all the stories in the book.... I don't think I'm a liar."[9]

These are astounding pronouncements, even for a fabulist as incorrigible as Mortenson. Scott Darsney, who trekked down from K2 with Mortenson and has remained his friend and loyal supporter throughout the ongoing scandal, told me more than once, without the slightest equivocation, that he was certain Mortenson didn't know Korphe even existed when the two of them flew home from Pakistan in 1993. In May 2010, Darsney stated the same thing during a formal interview with a senior CAI staff member—an interview that was videotaped for the CAI archives by Mike Simon, a videographer who has shot frequently for NBC News.

Remember, moreover, that the Korphe creation myth is just one of dozens of stories in *Three Cups of Tea* and *Stones into Schools* that are demonstrably false. These invented tales go far beyond the bounds of "literary license." In no sense can they be considered a "compression of events." They are lies, plain and simple, written with deliberate intent to deceive.

Mortenson suggested to Heard that the co-author of *Three Cups of Tea*, David Oliver Relin, shared responsibility for the book's inaccuracies. Perhaps, but it should be pointed out that Mortenson had been spinning yarns about the Korphe creation myth and his kidnapping by the Taliban to donors, journalists, and the CAI board of directors for at least five years before he met Relin.

On November 15, 2012, Relin committed suicide by lying down on railroad tracks as a train approached, positioning his body so the locomotive struck his head. In the aftermath of his death, Relin's wife told detectives that he'd been suffering from clinical depression and was taking several medications to alleviate it, with mixed results. "David had recently stopped taking an antidepressant—one that is notoriously difficult to get off of," she noted. "I have since learned that one of the possible side effects of the medication may be an increased risk of suicidal thoughts."

★ ★ ★

ON APRIL 16, 2011, a day after *60 Minutes* announced in a press release that "some of the most inspiring and dramatic stories in...*Three Cups of Tea* are not true," Viking (the imprint of the Penguin Group that published Mortenson's books) issued a statement declaring that it relied on its authors "to tell the truth, and they are contractually obligated to do so." On April 18, a day after the *60 Minutes* exposé was broadcast, Viking pledged in another statement, "*60 Minutes* is a serious news organization and in the wake of their report, Viking plans to carefully review the materials with the author."

A month after Viking made these statements, I wrote to the editor of Mortenson's books to ask "why Viking has said nothing further about the significant falsehoods presented as fact in both of Mortenson's books."

Two days later, I received a reply from Viking's director of publicity, who replied, "When Mortenson is recovered [he was suffering from serious health problems at the time] we will address any changes he feels need to be made."

Three years down the road, no one at Viking or the Penguin Group has said anything more about the lies in Mortenson's books or made further mention of its authors' obligations to be truthful. Notably, legal briefs filed by attorneys who defended Mortenson and Penguin in the class-action lawsuit over the veracity of his books did not claim that his books are factual accounts. Instead, these lawyers argued that the suit should be dismissed on constitutional grounds because "all of Penguin's alleged conduct is protected by the First Amendment," and therefore "Penguin owed no duty to publish accurate information."

Even though Penguin's lawyers declined to assert that Mortenson's books are truthful, Penguin continues to advertise and sell Mortenson's books as nonfiction. CAI also continues to promote Mortenson and his books as trustworthy. *Three Cups of Tea* no longer appears on the *New York Times* bestseller list, but it continues to sell briskly. Thanks to the curriculum still being promoted through CAI's Pennies for

Peace program, thousands of students are required to read the book every year in schools across North America.

The *Pennies for Peace Resource Guide* for grades 9 to 12 directs teachers to have students write an expository essay titled "Hero's Journey," in which they compare "Mortenson's journey in *Three Cups of Tea* with that of [a] hero from a specific work of fiction or mythology. For example, how does Mortenson's journey compare to that of Hercules?" An edition for young readers, *Listen to the Wind: The Story of Dr. Greg & Three Cups of Tea,* is assigned to teach students the difference between fiction and nonfiction. *The Pennies for Peace Resource Guide* for kindergarten through grade 4 urges teachers, "Tell students this is a true story (nonfiction) that takes place in a village called Korphe."

In 2011, the year Mortenson's misdeeds were exposed, donations to CAI dropped from $20.7 million to $15.6 million. In 2012, they declined much further, to $4.7 million, and then shrank to an estimated $3 million in 2013. That's a huge falloff, but it's still a lot of revenue for a charity as small as CAI, especially a charity embroiled in a high-profile scandal. This high level of continuing donations can likely be attributed in large part to the enduring emotional power of the counterfeit tales presented in *Three Cups of Tea*. Which isn't surprising, because according to the Montana attorney general's report, the book "was conceived as a fundraising tool":

> In addition to the production costs of approximately $367,000 for "Three Cups of Tea," since 2006 CAI has spent approximately $3.96 million buying copies of the books, which were distributed to libraries, schools, universities, the military, and other recipients to promote CAI and its mission.

Despite CAI's integral role in the conception, creation, and marketing of *Three Cups of Tea*, the board of directors has given no indication that CAI intends to do anything to inform potential donors that the book is substantially a work of fiction. Like Penguin, the CAI board apparently believes that Mortenson "has no duty to publish accurate information" and seems unconcerned about its complicity in Mortenson's acts of literary flimflam as long as the donations keep rolling in.

A strong argument can be made that the United States Constitution does indeed give Mortenson license to fill his books with lies, and similarly entitles Penguin to sell these false accounts as works of nonfiction. But even though Mortenson, Penguin, and the CAI board may have a legal right to snooker the public, the First Amendment doesn't absolve their ethical responsibility to be truthful. Mortenson and his enablers seem to have lost sight of this.

When David Starnes took over as the CAI executive director in March 2013, he made encouraging moves to clean up the organization. He placed a moratorium on constructing any more schools until CAI curbs graft, establishes better accounting practices, and determines how many existing schools are actually functioning. He also filed a lawsuit in Pakistan against ex–CAI program manager Ghulam Parvi for misusing CAI funds and illegally taking ownership of a very expensive four-story hostel in Skardu paid for by CAI donors. Starnes ostensibly had the power to hire and fire staff without interference from the board, and he repeatedly stated that he would have "zero tolerance for fraud, waste, and abuse." He promised that he would immediately terminate any CAI staff member caught using CAI funds for personal gain, no matter how small the sum. Starnes ran into unyielding resistance from the board of directors, however, and on May 13, 2014, CAI announced his resignation, "effective immediately," after barely a year on the job.

Meanwhile, the most brazen swindlers on the CAI team are still employed by the charity. Suleman Minhas remains in charge of CAI programs in Pakistan's Punjab Province, despite reportedly embezzling sums that may amount to hundreds of thousands of dollars. Even more to the point, Mortenson continues to be paid $169,000 per year and remains on the CAI board of directors, even after misappropriating $1.2 million from the organization. The fact that Starnes is gone while both Suleman and Mortenson remain on the CAI payroll suggests that a majority of the directors on the CAI board are staunch Mortenson devotees who won't consider forcing him out.

The board's unceasing loyalty to Mortenson is hard to figure, especially in light of recent actions taken by the boards of two other prominent nonprofits: The Somaly Mam Foundation and the Lance Armstrong Foundation.

In May 2014, *Newsweek* published an article by Simon Marks revealing that Somaly Mam, the Cambodian woman renowned for her crusade against sex trafficking, is a fraud. Marks discovered that Mam's claims to have been sold into slavery at age nine and forced to work as a child prostitute were untrue. The board of directors of her foundation retained a law firm that corroborated his allegations, after which Mam was compelled to resign.

In October 2012, when the board of the Lance Armstrong Foundation determined that Armstrong had lied about using performance-enhancing drugs, it not only forced him to resign, but changed the name of the organization to the Livestrong Foundation. As *New York Times* reporter Juliet Macur noted in her book *Cycle of Lies*, the decision to fire Lance wasn't simple:

> Armstrong had accomplished a lot with the Livestrong Foundation. He made it cool to survive cancer, and removed a stigma from those who had gone through months and years of pain and hospitalization. He personally donated $7 million, and the foundation raised a total of $500 million to help families touched by cancer.

When exposed as liars, both Armstrong and Mortenson blustered that their charities would fail without them. Armstrong sent an angry email to his board, calling them cowards for cutting him loose. But Armstrong's board—which includes individuals with whom he had close personal relationships—recognized that someone who had acted so disreputably for so many years needed to be jettisoned if the foundation hoped to rehabilitate its reputation and succeed in its mission. Mortenson's board, in striking contrast, remains obstinately in denial.

★ ★ ★

WHEN I FIRST MET Mortenson in 1997, I was impressed by his apparent sincerity, his humility, and his determination to build schools for the illiterate inhabitants of northern Pakistan. In 2001, John Marshall, the book critic for the *Seattle Post-Intelligencer*, wrote an article in which he quoted an email he'd received from Mortenson that affirmed how much Greg valued my support:

> Jon was one of the first people to appreciate the difficulty of our efforts in a remote region.... This writer I respect once told me that he was interested in our work because "actions speak louder than words."... Jon's acknowledgment of what we and the Balti villagers had accomplished with little outside support meant the world to me at the time.

Three years after Mortenson wrote these words, I learned he was misusing CAI funds. I was stunned. It felt like a personal betrayal. Demoralized, I faxed the letter to his office in which I lamented, "I have decided to suspend my financial support of CAI for the indefinite future." And then I walked away from both Mortenson and CAI, intending to never look back. In the spring of 2010, though, I finally brought myself to read *Three Cups of Tea*. By the time I'd finished the book, my internal bullshit detector had redlined, prompting me to contact several CAI employees and ex-employees to get their perspective on what the hell was going on at the organization.

I had taken for granted that CAI, having received the disquieting message I'd delivered six years earlier, would have fixed what was clearly broken. I discovered instead that the charity's problems had grown worse by an order of magnitude. It appeared as though Mortenson had been stricken with a virulent strain of megalomania, leading him to believe he was exempt from the ethical codes that guide the behavior of ordinary mortals and other charities. Like Lance Armstrong, he seemed to think he could lie about almost anything and get away with it.

Mortified that I had helped persuade many thousands of people to give their hard-earned money to a charlatan, and had done nothing more to correct my blunder than write a letter to CAI, I launched an exhaustive investigation of the charity to make amends. As my investigation gathered momentum and I came to understand just how dysfunctional the organization had become, I resolved to do my utmost to inform donors about the gravity of CAI's predicament. Millions of dollars donated to improve the lives of schoolchildren in Pakistan and Afghanistan had been used instead to enrich unscrupulous men. It was clear that Mortenson lacked both the skills and the desire to rectify what was wrong. When CAI staff pointed out corruption, he ignored them, and the CAI board of directors had long ago abdicated its responsibility to hold him accountable.

There was no reason to believe that writing another letter to Mortenson or the CAI board was going to be any more effective than the previous letter. So in April 2011, I published *Three Cups of Deceit,* and pledged to stay on the case until CAI was moving in the right direction. Sadly, more than three years later, the leaders of the organization continue to countenance Mortenson's lies and have been slow to enact crucial reforms. Hence this updated edition of my exposé.

CAI is at an existential crossroads. The need for the educational opportunities Mortenson pledged to deliver in Pakistan and Afghanistan is very real. While under his control, alas, CAI promised much more than it ever provided. Transforming the corrupt institutional culture that currently pervades CAI is going to be a long, challenging process at best, but the means exist to accomplish such a transformation. CAI currently has more than $16 million in the bank. All that's lacking is resolve.

The leaders of any charity determine the ethical standards of the entire organization, largely by the example of their own words and deeds. The CAI board of directors needs to stop covering up the deeply entrenched problems of the Mortenson era, and cease turning a blind eye to the fraudulent claims in his books and public statements. If the men and women who control CAI's fate hope to repair the devastation Mortenson's dishonesty has wrought, they must begin by acting honestly themselves.

As for Mortenson, he's a tragic and ultimately perplexing figure. Perhaps his efforts to conceal his lies by compulsively refashioning them into ever more convoluted lies can be explained by some emotional wound he suffered in the distant past. On the other hand, maybe he's simply playing the percentages. As P.T. Barnum noted, you really can fool some of the people all of the time. And "some" can be a big number. Mortenson is selling hope at a time when the prospects for much of the world are looking increasingly grim. It's counterfeit hope, for the most part, but it makes his supporters feel good about themselves, and that's reason enough for faithful donors to refrain from asking questions, cling stubbornly to the illusion, and keep sending checks to CAI. Think of it as a perverse variant of the placebo effect. Although this doesn't absolve Mortenson, it spreads the blame around, because in the final analysis, the only thing that allows people like him to remain in business is public demand for what they're hawking.

Jon Krakauer
October 2014

ENDNOTES

[1] According to *Three Cups of Tea* (pages 10 and 44), Mortenson was an accomplished mountaineer who, before attempting K2, had made "half a dozen successful Himalayan ascents," including climbs of 24,688-foot Annapurna IV and 23,389-foot Baruntse, both of which are in Nepal. In November 1990, Mortenson climbed 20,305-foot Island Peak, a minor summit in the Khumbu region of Nepal that is a very popular objective for trekkers and novice climbers. But there is no record in the *American Alpine Journal* (which documented all ascents of Annapurna IV and Baruntse prior to 1993) of Mortenson climbing Annapurna IV, Baruntse, or any other significant Himalayan mountain.

The *American Alpine Journal*'s record of Himalayan ascents is derived from the meticulous research of Elizabeth Hawley, the renowned Himalayan historian based in Kathmandu. According to Hawley, the fact that Mortenson's name is completely absent from her Himalayan database "does not prove he didn't go to either of these two mountains though it strongly suggests that he did not."

More than a year ago, Hawley's assistant, Billi Bierling, sent an email to Mortenson asking for information about his purported ascents of Annapurna IV and Baruntse. Although Mortenson's agent assured Bierling that Greg would provide the details she requested, "It never happened," Bierling told *Outside* magazine. When she sent a follow-up email, Mortenson didn't respond to that appeal, either.

[2] Mortenson's lies deeply offended Naimat Gul Mahsud. By falsely claiming to have been kidnapped by his hosts and threatened with death—an egregious contravention of *Pashtunwali*—Mortenson defamed the Mahsud clan. But aspects of Naimat Gul's own story turn out to be as fishy as Mortenson's. What Naimat Gul failed to disclose to Mortenson (and what Mortenson would likely never have known had it not been disclosed here) is that Naimat Gul was a professional con

artist. Although his late father, Nadir Khan, had been a famous war hero and the revered leader of one of the four Mahsud clans, Naimat Gul Mahsud "is just a criminal," says Hussein Mohammed (a pseudonym employed for the safety of the source), who has known Naimat Gul since he was a boy. "Cheating here, cheating there. Live this place, then move to some other place to cheat some other people." According to Mohammed, Naimat Gul has a long history of thievery, extortion, and counterfeiting. He was sentenced to life in prison for kidnapping a girl, but escaped from jail a year or two before meeting Mortenson, and has been on the lam ever since.

Naimat Gul committed most of his crimes in sprawl- ing cites such as Karachi, Dera Ismail Khan, and Peshawar. While he escorted Mortenson around the tribal areas, how- ever, Naimat Gul used Mortenson as an unwitting shill to pass counterfeit Pakistani rupees in the bazaars of North and South Waziristan. "Local people trusted Greg," says Moham- med, because "he is a foreigner and he would not cheat them." When this swindle proved successful, Naimat Gul attempted to profit in a grander fashion from Mortenson's visit by hatching an ill-advised blackmail scam: Naimat Gul falsely claimed that he had kidnapped Mortenson, then demanded a large ransom from wealthy members of the Mahsud clan—banking on the fact that if he'd actually kidnapped Mortenson, the authorities would hold Naimat Gul's entire family responsible.

When Naimat Gul tried to extort money from his rela- tives by purporting to have abducted Mortenson, his family was irate. If it were true, it would have brought disgrace to the entire clan. But instead of ceding to Naimat Gul's de- mands for hush money, his relatives called his bluff. Accord- ing to Hussein Mohammed, "Naimat Gul Mahsud's family told him, 'If you kidnap this man, and something happens to us or our businesses, if our jobs get in trouble due to you, then we will hold you responsible.'" After reflecting on the extremely harsh payback his enraged relatives were apt to deliver, Naimat Gul backed down and abandoned his scam.

When Mortenson flew home to Montana in the summer of 1996, he had no idea Naimat Gul Mahsud claimed to have kidnapped him. Ironically, Naimat Gul had no idea Mortenson would soon make the same spurious claim of abduction—a charge that millions of Americans now accept as fact.

3 In March 2004, the American Himalayan Foundation suspended Mortenson's stipend because he'd repeatedly failed to report how he had used funds from the Hoerni/Pakistan Fund, as required by the Internal Revenue Service, despite repeated requests to do so.

4 There is no evidence to suggest that Kevin Fedarko was aware of the falsehoods published in *Stones into Schools*. Because of the extraordinary deadline pressure he was under, he had no opportunity to fact-check what he ghostwrote for Mortenson, nor did his job description include that responsibility. Fedarko had no choice but to accept Mortenson's word that what he and Sarfraz Khan reported to him was accurate.

5 At the time, CAI was in fact not registered as a "charity NGO" in Afghanistan. It wasn't registered as such until 2008 (see *Stones into Schools*, pages 296–298).

6 By this point Mortenson knew that *60 Minutes* was preparing to broadcast an exposé of his misdeeds, and he was concerned that I might provide Steve Kroft with a recording of the interview I hoped to do with him.

7 http://www.slideshare.net/Byliner/greg-mortensons-route -from-k2-to-askole-1993

8 http://www.slideshare.net/Byliner1/route-by-which-mortenson -now-claims-he-reached-korphe-in-1993